The Smart Girl's Guide to

GETTING EVEN 5/07

For Norman + Barbara,
I f it weren't for
your generosity every
holiday season, I never
would've had time to
write this book cuz I'd
be out selling fake Rolex
watches on the corner to
earn extra cash.
Hope you enjoy the
read — if not? Sue Frank!
Love,
Alison Grabe

The Smart Girl's Guide to

GETTING EVEN

Alison Grambs

CITADEL PRESS
Kensington Publishing Corp.
www.kensingtonbooks.com

CITADEL PRESS BOOKS are published by

Kensington Publishing Corp.
850 Third Avenue
New York, NY 10022

All Kensington titles, imprints, and distributed lines are available at
special quantity discounts for bulk purchases for sales promotions,
premiums, fund-raising, educational, or institutional use. Special book
excerpts or customized printings can also be created to fit specific
needs. For details, write or phone the office of the Kensington special
sales manager: Kensington Publishing Corp., 850 Third Avenue,
New York, NY 10022, attn: Special Sales Department;
phone 1-800-221-2647.

First printing: April 2007

10   9   8   7   6   5   4   3   2   1

Printed in the United States of America

Library of Congress Control Number: 2006935127

ISBN-13: 978-0-8065-2808-3
ISBN-10: 0-8065-2808-7

For Mommy, Daddy, and Tommy

HOW TO USE THIS BOOK

Open the book and begin moving your eyes
from left to right. Turn the page. Repeat.

● ● ●

CONTENTS

INTRODUCTION

The Art of Revenge

• WHY YOU NEED TO SMARTEN UP, GIRL! •

You have spent the better half of your life saying "yes" when you wanted to say "no." Working so hard to please others, rather than yourself. You have allowed people to take advantage of you at every turn, from relatives and coworkers to lovers and friends. You are always there for your girlfriends in their time of need, but when you're having a bad day, you find yourself alone, curled up in a ball of depression, comforted only by a pint of freezer-burned ice cream and that rat thing you call a dog. You would never dream of telling your 486-pound girlfriend that she really shouldn't pursue a career as a trapeze artist, and yet, the tub of lard has no problem whatsoever pointing out that you're looking a bit chubby lately.

You've been working in the same under-appreciated, under-paid and under-whelming job for way too long, with annoying coworkers and a boss who doesn't respect you. You leave every family function with a severe case of explosive diarrhea, and are dating a guy who either spends all your money, cheats on you, or sucks in bed.

In short, you are a pushover.

The word "welcome" might as well be written across your forehead, because frankly, the only thing that distinguishes you from a doormat is that you have breasts.

Now you could just give up, drive to the nearest bridge, leap to your death, and end your suffering. But that's not your style. You're not a quitter. You're a fighter! And the very fact that you have purchased this book (or stolen it as the case may be) proves that you are ready, willing, and able to take your life back. (Besides, killing yourself means having to write a suicide note, make sure you have exact change for the bridge toll, blah, blah, blah. Who has time for that?)

Yes, it's payback time! You are going to bring out your inner Smart Girl and finally get even with everyone who has ever done you wrong. Even the telemarketer who bullied you into buying that "miracle" bagel slicer that does nothing miraculous at all. Revenge . . . ain't it sweet?

● THE "HOW WEAK AM I?" QUIZ ●

1 You and your siblings arrive for Thanksgiving dinner at Mom and Dad's, and your mother promptly begins bragging about your "brilliant" scientist sister, who discovered a cure for acne; your multilingual brother, who is solving international crises for the United Nations; and your twin cousins, who have apparently invented both a time machine and fat-free lard. Then, she points to you, sighs loudly, rolls her eyes, and remarks, "And then there's HER. The disappointment of the family." You:

    a. Whimper like a little baby, and offer to put yourself up for adoption.

    b. Inform the family that you, too, have discovered a cure for acne, solved international crises for the United Nations, and invented both a time machine and fat-free lard.

    c. Go stuff your face with lasagna.

    d. Pull out this book, which you have tucked in your homemade dish of candied yams, and turn to chapter 28, The Buttinksy Mother.

❷ You discover that your boyfriend has been cheating on you. He insists that the tryst "meant nothing," and begs for your forgiveness. You:

    a. Take him back. Because he's so cute when he cries.

    b. Take him back. Because he bought you a nice jacket for your birthday.

    c. Take him back. Because it's easier than being single.

    d. Pull out this book, which you have tucked inside the dozen roses he tried to bribe you with, and turn to chapter 1, The Cheater.

❸ A coworker has made a career of spreading nasty rumors about you in the office behind your back, and now everyone is convinced that you have not only slept with your boss, and the evening janitor, but stolen that packet of postage stamps out of the supply closet. None of the rumors are true (except for the stamp thing—you did take those). You:

    a. Ignore the rumors and hope they just go away.

    b. Sleep with the boss since everyone thinks you already have.

    c. Sleep with the janitor, since everyone already thinks you did.

    d. Pull out this book, which you have hidden inside the stolen packet of postage stamps, and turn to chapter 11, The Office Gossip.

❹ You and your boyfriend are engaged in er . . . well, um . . . ya know . . . coitus, when he suddenly suggests you try something different. Something that involves another woman named

Candy, a kitchen appliance, a hamster, and some cheese. You are very uncomfortable with this new bedroom proposition, but your lover is insistent. You:

    a. Look for the nearest electrical outlet and help Candy remove her hair extensions.

    b. Pretend you are enjoying the company of the hamster and suggest bringing a ferret next time.

    c. Get out the video camera so he can show all his friends what he did.

    d. Pull out this book, which you have tucked underneath Candy's hair extensions, and turn to chapter 5, The Bad in Bed Dude.

5 Despite years of dedicated service to your job you have just been passed over for yet another promotion. The big raise, the office with a view, the potted plant? They all went to someone newer, younger, and dumber than yourself. You:

    a. Send the boss a thank-you card for just being a part of your life.

    b. Send the newer, younger, and dumber coworker a "Congratulations!" card.

    c. Apologize to the entire office for not being up to snuff, and offer to work for free for the next year.

    d. Pull out this book, which you have tucked in your desk drawer, and turn to chapter 17, Mr. Boss.

6 You are utterly exhausted after a stressful day at work and want to do nothing more than take a hot bubble bath and crawl into bed for a night of mindless television. Just as your head hits the pillow, the phone rings. It's your self-centered girlfriend on the line. She has just been dumped for the eighth time in seven days and wants to tell you all about it. You:

    a. Turn off the television and tell her to start at the very beginning of the story.

    b. Press the MUTE button on the television, and tell her to start at the very beginning.

    c. Press the MUTE button on the television, but switch on the thing that gives you the English subtitles, and tell her to start at the very beginning.

    d. Pull out this book, which you have sitting next to the remote, and turn to chapter 24, The "It's All About Me" Friend.

7 You and a coworker have been working on a project together for several months, and the day finally arrives to present your team's ideas to the client. Lo and behold, on the day of the presentation you overhear your coworker take full credit for your ideas. You:

    a. Excuse yourself to go cry in the restroom. Then return as if nothing happened.

    b. Let her get the credit. After all, there's no "I" in "team."

    c. Hand her your paycheck from now on. Clearly, she earned it.

    d. Pull out this book, which you have tucked into your portfolio, and turn to chapter 10, The Office Pet.

8 You and your best friend are on a gal pal cruise in the Caribbean. You didn't want to go, but she begged you, swearing it would be the best vacation ever. Since leaving port you have suffered through a vicious sunburn and paid way too much for watered down drinks. And worst of all, your girlfriend has ditched you every night for some creepy guy with too much hair on his back and too little hair on his head.

    a. Begin planning your next vacation with the slut.

    b. Hurl yourself over the edge of the Lido Deck and feed yourself to the sharks.

    c. Take advantage of the alone time to catch up on some masturbation.

    d. Pull out this book, which you have tucked inside your vibrator, and turn to page chapter 26, The Flake.

9 It is a rainy Sunday afternoon and you are enjoying a movie at the local theater. Not five minutes into the movie you have a couple in front of you chatting loudly, a fat guy behind you panting into his gallon tub of popcorn, and a woman to your left who keeps putting her arm on your armrest. In short, the movie is being ruined for you. You:

    a. Leave the theater and try not to think about the money you just wasted.

    b. Chew on your popcorn extra loud to drown out all the interference.

    c. Move to another seat.

    d. Pull out this book, which you have tucked inside your tub of popcorn, and turn to Part Five, The General Public.

10 Your cheapskate best friend and you have just exchanged holiday gifts. You gave her a $100 gift certificate to the best spa in town; and she presented you with a book you gave her for Christmas two years ago! Only now it has a giant booger stain on the cover. You:

a. Thank her profusely for the book, wipe off the booger and race home to read it.

b. Thank her profusely, wipe off the booger, and donate the book to the local library.

c. Thank her profusely, don't wipe the booger off, and read it.

d. Pull out this book, which you have tucked inside your own booger-filled nose, and turn to chapter 20, The Mooch.

Scoring: If you answered anything but "d" to any of these questions, you are a putz. A nincompoop. A complete and utter pushover. But it's not your fault. As a pushover, you have been conditioned to accept defeat by the bullies in your life. No more, though! This book is going to teach you how to take back your life.

PART ONE

Love

Two Mr. Wrongs Make a Mr. Right . . . Enough

• • •

Ten Signs You're a Pushover in Love

1. You allow your lover to nap during foreplay.

2. Your best date involved a Laundromat and a roll of quarters.

3. Your boyfriend spends the holidays with his wife and kids.

4. The homemade porno you donated to the local video store has been shelved in the "Horror" section.

5. You can't remember the last time a guy paid for dinner.

6. You consider a romance with the toll booth taker on the turnpike out of reach.

7. You've had more alien encounters than orgasms.

8. You are in a committed relationship with a Death Row inmate.

9. Your boyfriend took out a restraining order against you.

10. You're considering becoming a lesbian.

He sure seemed like Mr. Right those first couple of dates, didn't he? He was cute, charming, smart enough to keep you interested, but not so smart that you felt intimidated. He bought you thoughtful gifts "just because," and tongue-kissed without slobbering all over your mouth. Heck, he even hit it off with your mother! And before you knew it, you caught yourself thinking, *Self, this guy could be the one!* But just when you had rehearsed squealing the word "Yes!" to perfection . . . just when you began subscribing to bridal magazines and fantasizing about three-tiered cakes . . . just when you had committed to shaving your legs on a regular basis for this guy . . . POW! Mr. Right began demonstrating signs of (gasp!) imperfection. They manifested themselves in various ways—deviant behavior, selfishness, neglect of personal hygiene. And before you knew it you were emotionally committed to a big, fat Mr. Wrong.

Don't worry. It's not your fault.

There are a lot of them out there. Heck, you wouldn't be a real woman if you didn't have at least one Mr. Wrong on your record. From cheaters and cheapskates, to couch potatoes and lousy lovers, these nitwits wiggle their way into your heart, suck you into their lives, and then poop all over you.

However, despite his myriad flaws, you still love this shmuck. And that's okay. Even the smartest of Smart Girls remains powerless over the gravitational pull of her heart strings. You can't help whom you fall in love with, even if the object of your adoration has a fear of commitment or could be gay. But that doesn't mean you settle for Mr. Wrong. No, No! You have too much self-respect for that.

Instead, by employing some of the following revenge tactics, you can turn that Mr. Wrong into a true Mr. Right. Basically scare him into being the man he was meant to be. It may not be romantic . . . but neither is marrying a guy who is permanently attached to the sofa cushions.

CHAPTER 1

The Cheater

(Latin: *Fornicatorus extracurricularus*)

● OBSERVED BEHAVIOR IN NATURAL HABITAT ●

This creature sleeps, breathes, and eats through his genitalia, slithering about the female population like a snake in a desert sand pit. He is armed with two cell phones but gives you the number for only one and calls you by the wrong name during sex. He takes more "overnight business trips" than the CEO of any Fortune 500 company and inevitably returns from them smelling of perfume you do not wear. In short, he is a scumbag of the most vile kind.

● OFTEN HEARD SAYING ●

"Man, I can't believe I have to take another business trip to the Bahamas . . ."

"I would never cheat on you."

"It didn't mean anything."

"Those condoms? Er . . . well, er . . . I use those to keep my pencils dry."

"I thought of you the whole time."

• WHY YOU MUST TAKE ACTION •

Craving some chlamydia? Gunning for gonorrhea? Salivating for syphilis? Unless these tasty delights are on your menu du jour, you must knock the cheat out of the Cheater before he gives your gynecologist something to chortle about at lunch with the other vagina doctors. He is not only making a fool of you, but endangering your life with every stolen kiss (and whatever else he's getting on the side). Stop his sneaky ways fast or you will spend the rest of your romance wondering if you were the last person to see him naked. And let's be honest . . . you weren't.

• IT'S REVENGE TIME! •

Exacting revenge on the Cheater is simply a matter of outsmarting his penis. (And we know that little thang ain't much competition, right?) Because the Cheater relies on his ability to juggle two separate lives, you, Smart Girl, must make his parallel lives collide at every turn. Interfere with his extracurricular activities every chance you get, until the only cheatin' this jerk can do is on his income taxes!

THE SUBTLE APPROACH

❶ *An Itch in Time Saves Nine:* It's pretty hard to cheat on someone when you can't stop scratching your balls. That's the theory behind this nifty little revenge device. Go to the local novelty shop and purchase some itching powder. (If money is an issue, talcum powder with a little chili powder, black pepper, and Greek sea salt will suffice.) Dust his underwear with the powder, and send him off for his next "business trip." The only itch he'll be scratching is the one between his ball sack.

❷ *For a Good Time Call . . .* Gather up the Cheater's matchbox collection—you know, the ones slutty women hand him at those slut-filled bars he claims he never goes to. Change a few digits on each of the phone numbers you find scribbled inside. Turn that 6 into an 8, that 4 into a 9, a 1 into a 7 here and there.

Before long the Cheater will get so frustrated trying to make a booty call to "Crystal" but getting Benny's Deli instead, he'll just give up and stay home with you. That's when you make him play a Scrabble marathon. And look at baby pictures of you.

❸ *Valentine's Day:* Purchase a generic Valentine's Day card right before the big holiday arrives and doctor the handwriting to resemble his. Address it to "Sue" and sign it from the Cheater. Then mail it to yourself and act devastated when you open it. "OH MY GOD! How could you do this to me! You're seeing another woman?!" Chances are the Cheater is banging someone named Sue and will inadvertently accept blame for the mishap. And only a pound a week of Godiva chocolates and a foot rub every night will gain your forgiveness.

THE NOT-SO-SUBTLE APPROACH

❶ *Crying Wolf:* Whenever you suspect the Cheater is up to no good dial his cell phone and scream: "OH MY GOD, HONEY! Your mother has just been raced to the hospital for emergency surgery. They're not sure she's going to make it!" No matter how many times you ring this false alarm, the Cheater's conscience will always get the better of him, forcing him to stop whatever . . . or whomever . . . he is doing, get dressed, and race to the hospital every single time—with blue balls—nonetheless.

❷ *Dial 1–800–IHVNSTD:* Call the Cheater's mistress and identify yourself as a member of the United States Health Department. Inform her that she is on the list of sexual partners said Cheater has asked be informed of his herpes diagnosis. She'll be rethinking this tryst, and that cold sore on her lip, in no time.

❸ *Crossing Over:* Hire a cross-dresser to seduce the Cheater. The more "she" looks like Pamela Anderson, the better. When the Cheater realizes that the nice piece of ass he got also had a pair of cajones he'll be too shell shocked to ever cheat on you again. Problem solved. (At least your problem . . . your boyfriend is gonna need some serious therapy.)

THE YOU'RE GOING TO HELL APPROACH

1. *Happy Father's Day:* Borrow a girlfriend's baby for the afternoon and bring it home. Right before the Cheater is due to arrive home from one of his overnight "business trips," place the baby in a bassinet on his front porch with a note attached that reads, "Happy Father's Day. He's yours." Sign it from "Your Mistress." That's an awful lot of phone calls he'll have to make.

2. *The Staple of Life:* Choose the most splinter-filled portion of your bed's headboard and staple the Cheater's penis to it. He won't be sleeping around on you anytime soon. As a matter of fact he won't be leaving the bedroom anytime soon.

3. *Call 1–800–IMDEAD:* Whenever one of the Cheater's mistresses calls looking for him, weep into the phone, "I'm sorry to tell you this, but he passed away." This pretty much guarantees they won't be calling back anytime soon.

• TOP THREE GIFTS TO GIVE THE CHEATER •

1. *Fatal Attraction*—The Collector's Edition.

2. A poster of John Wayne Bobbitt.

3. Penicillin.

CHAPTER 2

The Unemployed Couch Potato

(Latin: *Maximus loserus*)

● OBSERVED BEHAVIOR IN NATURAL HABITAT ●

This creature was voted "Most Likely to Do Nothing" in high school and spends his days fulfilling that prophecy reclining on the sofa like a beached whale, watching daytime television and stuffing Doritos into his mouth. He has five-o'clock shadow all hours of the day and a family who denies his existence. He justifies his failure to hold down a job with that ever-annoying excuse, "I'm working on a great deal" and has borrowed enough money from you to clear the national debt. In short, he serves little to no purpose on the planet other than keeping the sofa cushions warm.

● OFTEN HEARD SAYING ●

"Where's the remote?"

"Yeah, yeah. I'll get to the dishes next week."

"Oh my God . . . WHERE'S the remote?!"

"I just haven't found a job that makes use of all my skills yet."

"Zzzzzzzzzz."

• WHY YOU MUST TAKE ACTION •

The first problem with the Unemployed Couch Potato is that his lazy butt has become permanently imprinted on your sofa cushion. The second problem is that his latency is highly contagious, and thereby a hazard to your ambitious self. Studies show that the more you are around a loser, the more normal their loser-ness becomes to you. Before you know it you've become a loser yourself. If you don't kick his fleshy butt off the couch and into gear, you will end up going to your thirty-year high school reunion with nothing more to show for your life than the ability to recite the *TV Guide*.

• IT'S REVENGE TIME! •

A body in motion is a body that can do the dishes and make the bed. A body at rest is pretty much only good for concealing that nasty cranberry juice stain on the couch. Take your pick.

THE SUBTLE APPROACH

1. *The Boob Tube Block:* Every five minutes or so step directly in front of the television to ask stupid questions like, "Have you seen the salt?" and "Do I look fat in these flannel pajamas?" It is best to time these interference runs to coincide with say, the final few minutes of a major college football game—preferably one on which he has a lot of money riding.

2. *The Cover-Up:* If the Unemployed Couch Potato insists on making himself part of the furniture, then put his dead weight to good use. Smack out dusty pillows against his back. Balance your game of Solitaire on his belly. Encourage short guests to use him as a booster seat during dinner. There are all sorts of wonderful uses for a loser! And you can exploit all of them.

3. *Would You Like Scrambled Eggs with That?* Call the cable company and have all the Unemployed Couch Potato's favorite

television channels scrambled: ESPN, The Playb[
The Sumo Wrestling Channel, The Disgusting Thin[
Network. He'll have nothing to watch but that PBS [
how to knit tissue box covers. That might get him mo[

THE NOT-SO-SUBTLE APPROACH

1. *Sew What?* While the Unemployed Couch Potato lays napping on the couch, carefully and quietly sew the seam of his pants to the sofa cushions. Then place the remote on the opposite side of the living room, turn off the television, and leave for six hours.

2. *And You Are?* Go online and register his cell phone number with tons of telemarketers and sales websites. Then tell the Unemployed Couch Potato he is the finalist in a radio sweepstakes to win $5 million dollars. He'll spend all day answering the calls, just hoping the next one is the one announcing he is the lucky winner.

3. *The Superbawl:* "Accidentally" tape over all the Unemployed Couch Potato's football games with re-runs of *E! True Hollywood Story.*

THE YOU'RE GOING TO HELL APPROACH

1. *Honey, I'm Home!* The Unemployed Couch Potato relishes the eight hours a day he has at home by himself to do important things like flip his body from the right side of the sofa to the left. So, imagine how frustrated he'll be when you inform him that you have quit your job and will now be spending every single waking hour at home. On the couch. Right next to him. From now on, he must share the sofa and his Doritos and his Oreo cookies and the throw pillows and, worst of all, the remote with the likes of you! He'll be looking for a job in no time.

❷ *The Angelina:* Make like Angelina Jolie and adopt a bunch of needy babies from third world countries. Leave the Unemployed Couch Potato at home alone with them all day. Come the third day or so he'll be more than ready to start looking for a job.

❸ *While You Were Sleeping:* Wait until the Unemployed Couch Potato falls asleep. Then call 9–1–1. When the paramedics arrive, point to the "dead body" on the couch. There are only so many times the Unemployed Couch Potato will put up with being zipped into a body bag and buried alive before he'll start checking out the Want Ads.

• TOP THREE GIFTS TO GIVE THE UNEMPLOYED COUCH POTATO •

❶ The entire collection of Anthony Robbins motivational tapes.

❷ A drool cup.

❸ A book . . . with no pictures in it.

CHAPTER 3

The Jealous Fiend

(Latin: *Doofus erectus*)

• OBSERVED BEHAVIOR IN NATURAL HABITAT •

This creature will punch the mailman's lights out for looking at you one second too long. He hits the REDIAL button on the phone after you make a call, follows you to and from work, and assumes that you want to sleep with every man you encounter . . . including the one-armed hot dog cart vendor on the corner by your office. If you dare to wear eye shadow in public, the Jealous Fiend accuses you of "whoring yourself out," and on more than one occasion, he has demanded you wear overalls and a burka for Girls Night Out. And burkas sooo dry out your scalp!

• OFTEN HEARD SAYING •

"Where were you this morning?"

"Where were you this afternoon?"

"Where were you tonight?"

"Where are ya gonna be tomorrow morning?"

"Where are ya gonna be tomorrow around, say, 4:15 p.m.?"

• WHY YOU MUST TAKE ACTION •

While it is very nice to have a guy want you all to himself, there is a fine line between the normal "I'd prefer you not show so much cleavage in church, dear" kind of boyfriend jealousy and the, "If I see you looking at that male porpoise with those come hither eyes one more time, I'll slit your throat" kind of boyfriend jealousy. Trust is the bedrock of any healthy relationship. If the Jealous Fiend doesn't believe that when you say you're going to the corner to pick up a gallon of milk, you are, in fact, going to the corner to pick up a gallon of milk—well, then, what is the point of dating him? (Not to mention your Cheerios are going to taste pretty dry all by their lonesome.)

• IT'S REVENGE TIME! •

As any shrink can tell you for $50 per minute, the Jealous Fiend suffers from extreme feelings of inadequacy (insert sad violin music here). And his fears of abandonment and loss have become a veritable noose around your neck. But despite the fact his psychological hang-ups spelled out disaster for you as a couple, they are a godsend when it comes to getting even with the dude. The more fragile his ego, the more fun you will have torturing him into submission!

THE SUBTLE APPROACH

1. *Copycat:* Sift through the Hollywood tabloids and cut out photographs of all the hottest male celebrities with their supermodel girlfriends. Take these, along with some passport-size photos of yourself, to the local copy shop. Superimpose your head onto the models' bodies. Soon you'll have a collection of candid shots of you frolicking on a Hawaiian beach with Heath Ledger. Sipping Chablis in Southern France with Johnny Depp. Motorcycling with Brad Pitt in the Smoky Mountains. Then slip all the new photos into a scrapbook and conveniently leave the album on the living room coffee table for the Jealous Fiend to come across.

② *The Name Game:* "Accidentally" call him by your ex's name.

③ *Feeling a Little Randy:* Every chance you get talk about your new friend, Randy. "Randy's so good-looking!" "I can't wait to see Randy!" "Randy gives such great hugs!" Then dress up in your highest heels and your lowest-cut blouse, and head out to meet your new friend, Randy. The Jealous Fiend will inevitably follow you only to discover that Randy is a 300-pound female friend you met in your pot holder–making class.

THE NOT-SO-SUBTLE APPROACH

① *The Hell's Angle:* Accompany the Jealous Fiend to the skankiest diner in town. When he comes back from using the restroom point to the largest, meanest, and most heavily armed Hell's Angel in the joint and scream at the top of your lungs, "That wimp just made a pass at me! Go defend my honor, honey! You can take him!" He'll be beaten into a raw pulp by the entire biker gang before your pancakes arrive.

② *Jack and the Beanstalker:* Invent a stalker and give the Jealous Fiend a vague description of the man who is following your every move: "average height . . . probably either white, Hispanic, or Czech," speaks with "a voice." The Jealous Fiend will spend all his free time trying to track down this imaginary white/Czech, not-quite-short, not-quite-tall dude with "a voice," which gives you some free time to take in a museum or two.

③ *Love Is for the Birds:* Get all gussied up one night. The whole shebang. Fake eyelashes, expensive perfume, and tight clothes that show off every curve of your body. Then inform the Jealous Fiend that you will be "going out" for the evening. He'll be so suspicious of your odd behavior that he will inevitably follow you. Right to the park bench where you will spend the next twelve hours feeding pigeons and reading the paper. The poor shmuck will sit there all day expecting your date to show up any second. Which, of course, he won't.

THE YOU'RE GOING TO HELL APPROACH

1. *The Chick Flick:* Become a lesbian. Unless he is willing to grow boobies and trade in his boxers for a thong, the Jealous Fiend won't even try to compete for your affections now. Heck, you're not even playing with the same equipment anymore! This is a game he simply cannot win.

2. *Ransom Acts of Kindness:* Disappear suddenly. After about a week mail a ransom note to the Jealous Fiend from your captors stating that unless he answers your kidnappers' demands, you will be used as a sex slave by your captors. The demand, of course, is that he Federal Express a photo of himself dressed as a baby, complete with diaper, bonnet, and thumb-sucking pose, out to every person in the phone book whose last name has the letter "e" in it.

3. *Homely Sweet Home:* If you need some relief from the Jealous Fiend's constant inquisitions and harassing phone calls, you can simply make yourself as unattractive as possible. Stop wearing makeup and brushing your teeth. Shave your head. Grow out your toenails. Put on 400 pounds and forsake bathing. Pretty soon he'll be begging other guys to take you off his hands.

• TOP THREE GIFTS TO GIVE THE JEALOUS FIEND •

1. A collection of poems you've written about other boyfriends.

2. Underwear with no easy-access pee flap.

3. A weekend getaway for three in the Poconos.

CHAPTER 4

The Cheapskate

(Latin: *Pincherus of the pennyus*)

If you were lying on the side of the road bleeding to death and you called this creature for help, he would tell you wait until after 9 p.m. to avoid cellular roaming charges, then hang up on you. He's too stingy to spring for cable television, only orders food off the Dollar Menu at Wendy's, and turns his underwear inside out so he can wear them two days in a row. His bathroom is stocked with generic brand toothpaste and shampoo, and you are quite certain that the birthday card he gave you is the same one you sent him a year ago.

• OFTEN HEARD SAYING •

"Did you bring the calculator?"

"Let's go Dutch."

"Wow, that hot dog was expensive."

"Let's go with the cheaper one."

"Can I borrow some cash?"

• WHY YOU MUST TAKE ACTION •

Do you work your fingers to the bone for that measly paycheck each week just so you can give your hard-earned cash away? Of course not. It is essential that you fight back against this creature before your bank account suffers. You cannot afford to split one more dinner bill with this miser, or charge one more vacation to your credit card. Every day you let the Cheapskate use generic-brand condoms and stiff a waitress out of her tip brings you one step closer to wearing a wedding ring made of tinfoil. If you do not take action immediately, you can kiss the good life adios (that's Spanish for "good-bye" . . . or Swahili for "pork") . . . and say hello to a life spent waiting six months to see the latest movies on DVD and sleeping on a mattress picked out of the trash.

• IT'S REVENGE TIME! •

Go to your purse and take out your wallet . . . seriously . . . go! And no stopping in the kitchen for a Mallowmar. Now count the money you have inside that wallet. Easy enough, right? Why? BECAUSE YOU DON'T HAVE ANY! The Cheapskate is sucking you dry. Now take out a calculator and all the receipts you've collected since your first date with this miser. Add up everything he has cost you over the years. Then follow these steps to get some payback.

THE SUBTLE APPROACH

① *Oooops! I Did It Again!* Conveniently leave your wallet at home every time you and the Cheapskate go out. He'll be forced to foot the bill everywhere . . . or get arrested trying not to!

② *Don't Be So Shellfish:* The next time the Cheapskate drags you to "Hector's Road Side Seafood Truck" out on Highway 62 for Valentine's Day, suck down all the rotten oysters you can. Food poisoning will set in within the half hour, just in time for you to get back into his car and "accidentally" puke all over his front seats. Chances are he'll let you pick the restaurant from then on.

③ *Fuel's Gold:* In the dark of night siphon the gas out of his car with a straw. Then pour that gas into your gas tank. This will save you a bundle in fuel expenses. (But it will also give you really bad breath so make sure to suck on a mint after.)

THE NOT-SO-SUBTLE APPROACH

① *I'll Be Right Back . . . Not!* Invite the Cheapskate out for a meal at a fancy restaurant, your treat. Order up all the most expensive items on the menu, then eat them. (Even if you don't like imported chilled monkey brains in hollandaise sauce.) When the bill arrives, politely excuse yourself to go to the ladies' room. Climb out the restroom window, hail a cab, and go home.

② *Re-Gift the He-Gift:* Next time you spend the night at the Cheapskate's pad, filch some things from his home that he is not likely to miss. That still as yet wrapped candle he got from his great aunt for Christmas. That shoehorn his brother gave him that he never used. That paring knife and spatula set he won in that raffle for the Special Olympics. Bring these items home, polish them up with some glass cleaner, and wrap them up in pretty paper with pretty bows to match. Voilà! Now you have gifts for every occasion, including President's Day. And with the money left over can buy you some new shoes. (Or maybe a paring knife of your very own!)

③ *The Gift of Nothing:* Give him a $100 gift certificate to a store that does not exist.

THE YOU'RE GOING TO HELL APPROACH

① *In the Dog House:* Adopt a really, really sick dog from the local pound, one with an incurable, but nonfatal disease that must be managed with expensive medications and costly visits to the vet on a regular basis. Present the sick dog to the Cheapskate as a gift. And this is important . . . name the dog after his mother. That way he won't dare get rid of little sick Fido.

2 *Quit Your Renting and Raving:* Rent out your apartment for a month without the Cheapskate's knowledge. Tell him it's being exterminated or something like that. He'll be forced to let you stay with him until you can safely return to your own pad. All the while, you will be turning a handsome little profit with that extra income he knows nothing about. Oh, and while you're at his place, make sure to call Ethiopia once a day on his cell phone, during peak hours, of course. Order some Pay-Per-View shows off the premium channels while you're at it.

3 *The Live Organ Donor:* Drug the Cheapskate. Then remove one of his kidneys with a pair of salad tongs, sell the kidney on the black market, and use the profits to take a nice cruise somewhere sunny and warm.

• TOP THREE GIFTS TO GIVE THE CHEAPSKATE •

1 A *Christmas Carol*—The Collector's Edition.

2 A coupon for a massage with a one-armed midget.

3 A piggy bank that only takes Canadian pennies.

CHAPTER 5

The Bad in Bed Dude

(Latin: *Erectilus dysfunctionus*)

● OBSERVED BEHAVIOR IN NATURAL HABITAT ●

A veritable lovemaking disaster, this creature is about as sexy in the bedroom as a bag of toenail clippings. His "hot moves" include flopping up and down against your body like a dying fish, drooling all over your face, and poking you in all the wrong places with all the wrong things. You have had to fake so many orgasms with him that you are up for an Oscar this year.

● OFTEN HEARD SAYING ●

"Was it good for you?"

"Want to do it again?"

"Man, that was an exhausting three seconds!"

"Did you hit it?"

"Uh, I'm . . . uh, finished already. Sorry."

● WHY YOU MUST TAKE ACTION ●

Would you invest your money in a three-legged race horse? Or buy a house with no roof on it? Of course not. But devoting yourself to the Bad in Bed Dude is pretty much like doing either of those things. Girl, the purpose of having a boyfriend is to reap the rewards of limitless romance and mind-blowing sex. (And yes, if we're being completely honest here, so that there is someone available to sign for Federal Express deliveries when you're not home.) But the Bad in Bed Dude leaves you contemplating celibacy, which means you might as well trade in that Victoria's Secret negligee for a nun's habit.

• IT'S REVENGE TIME •

It is bad enough having to put up with a boyfriend's snoring in bed. But his sexual shortcomings to boot? Hardly seems fair, right? You should be relishing multiple orgasms, not praying for a monsoon to sweep the Bad in Bed Dude off your limp body and into the sea. If he won't take the usual hints, you have to hint louder.

THE SUBTLE APPROACH

1. *The Mother Load:* Every time you and the Bad in Bed Dude are engaged in what he calls lovemaking—but you call a nap—bring up his mother. While he is pumping away, suddenly say something like, "By the way, I forgot to tell you. Your mother called. She wants to know if we're coming over for Thanksgiving this year." He'll find it very difficult to concentrate after that, and hopefully, just give up.

2. *On a Waterbed of Roses:* Swap out your standard mattress for a waterbed. The more seasick the Bad in Bed Dude gets, the more often you can avoid bad sex.

3. *A Penny Shaved Is a Penny Earned:* While frighteningly simple, this tactic is highly effective. Stop shaving. The longer your pubic, armpit, and leg hair grows, the less the Bad in Bed Dude will want to forage through it.

THE NOT-SO-SUBTLE APPROACH

1. *The Cost of Inflation:* Set up an inflatable doll in place of your own body in the bed. Dress it in a slutty negligee and spritz it with your perfume. A few glasses of wine, some soft candlelight, and Barry White's Greatest Hits echoing through the stereo, chances are the Bad in Bed Dude will be none the wiser when he's done . . . about three minutes later.

2. *Hooker, Line, and Sinker:* Begin charging the Bad in Bed Dude per minute. Yes, this borders on prostitution, but you have to get something out of this arrangement, too.

3. *The Yeast Always Rises:* Contract a yeast infection. (You can do this by wearing a wet bathing suit under your jeans.) The Bad in Bed Dude will steer clear of a woman leaking a frothy, yellowish discharge.

THE YOU'RE GOING TO HELL APPROACH

1. *Congratulations! It's a Boy:* Get pregnant every time you have sex. That'll discourage the Bad in Bed Dude real fast.

2. *The Threesome of All Its Parts:* If the Bad in Bed Dude insists on having sex, you're going to up the ante and suggest a threesome. Because he is a man, he will be up for this . . . literally. But instead of inviting some hot stripper home, bring to bed the, um, er, largest and most experienced male Internet porno star you can rent by the hour. This way you will be guaranteed at least one good romp, and the Bad in Bed Dude might pick up a trick or two . . . after he gets over crying in the corner all by his lonesome, of course.

3. *Play Dead:* About twenty minutes before the Bad in Bed Dude is due to enter the boudoir, slather that white clown face

makeup all over your face and upper body until your skin has a pasty, corpse-like look to it. Then stand in front of the air conditioner so your skin becomes cold to the touch. Then lay in the bed with the covers up to your chin, close your eyes, and tense all your muscles to mimic the onset of rigor mortis. Hold your breath and keep your abdomen very, very still. The Bad in Bed Dude will slip into bed to find his beloved has sadly passed away. When he runs to call the ambulance, revive yourself. "It's a miracle! I saw the light!" Do this every time he attempts to have sex, and soon enough, he'll just settle for masturbation like the rest of the male population.

• TOP THREE GIFTS TO GIVE THE BAD IN BED DUDE •

1. A Kama Sutra calendar.

2. A Kama Sutra book.

3. A Kama Sutra tea pot cozy.

CHAPTER 6

Mr. Sexually Ambiguous

(Latin: *Homo sapien*)

● OBSERVED BEHAVIOR IN NATURAL HABITAT ●

This creature is a walking dichotomy. He is traditionally "manly" in that he holds the door for you, but "unmanly" in that he expresses no interest in sports. He can assemble even the most complex of IKEA furniture in a single bound, but jams on air guitar to Broadway show tunes. He can get a broken-down car running like new in a matter of seconds, but runs away crying at the sight of a mouse. He is incredible in bed, but logs in more time at the manicure salon than you do. Your mother tells you you're lucky to have a guy with such a flair for designing window treatments, and your friends are jealous of your modern, metrosexual boyfriend, who always looks and smells fabulous. You know you should be thrilled, but sometimes you can't help but wonder . . . is he gay?

● OFTEN HEARD SAYING ●

"Honey, where's the latest issue of *Better Homes and Gardens*? I wanted to take it into the bathroom with me."

"Hey, why don't we invite your friend Susan over for dinner? Oh, and her boyfriend, George, the football player with the big pectoral muscles?"

"Do these jeans make me look fat?"

"I love rainbows!"

"Liza Minnelli in concert! I must be dreaming!"

• WHY YOU MUST TAKE ACTION •

There is a big difference between a guy being in touch with his feminine side and a guy just being downright feminine. Love is confusing enough—the last thing you should have to worry about is whether this guy is even playing for the right team. Because let's face it, while there is nothing wrong with being gay, you need to date a guy who is attracted to you . . . not your brother.

• IT'S REVENGE TIME! •

The key to handling Mr. Sexually Ambiguous is to suppress his feminine side as best you can. Remind him that he has testicles, not breasts.

THE SUBTLE APPROACH

❶ *Disorderly Conduct:* Sneak into Mr. Sexually Ambiguous's dresser drawer and wreak havoc on his organizational skills. Crumple up all his shirts, mismatch his Polo socks, and *gasp!* un-color-coordinate his tie collection. The first step toward making him a real man is forcing him to live like a slob.

❷ *Straight Eye for the Queer Guy:* Remove all the Monet posters from Mr. Sexually Ambiguous's abode and replace them with die cast models of hot rod cars. Swap out his Cuisinart food processor for that *Dukes of Hazard* collectors edition toaster you found at the flea market. Toss his DVD of *The Wizard of Oz* in the trash and replace it with *Little Oral Annie.* Hang some shotguns on the wall, and scatter his dirty underwear all over the living room couch along with some empty beer cans and stale pizza. An inflatable doll in the likeness of Pamela Anderson wouldn't hurt either.

❸ *Real Men Don't Eat Quiche:* Take Mr. Sexually Ambiguous out for a romantic dinner at a French restaurant and tell him to order whatever his heart desires. If he goes for the Quiche Lorraine, stab him in the eye with your fork. Do this every time he tries to order Quiche Lorraine.

THE NOT-SO-SUBTLE APPROACH

❶ *Somewhere Over the Rainbow:* Tape over Mr. Sexually Ambiguous's Judy Garland movie marathon with something really manly like the Superbowl or NASCAR.

❷ *The Charity Case:* Donate Mr. Sexually Ambiguous's entire wardrobe to a local homeless outreach program. The designer socks, the pink polo shirts, the silk shirts. Yes, the hip huggers, too. Replace his wardrobe with straight guy essentials like baggy jeans from 1988, construction boots with dirt on them. Oh, and tattered pairs of tighty whities with poop streaks on them.

❸ *Designer Sports Wear:* Sew sports team logos on all Mr. Sexually Ambiguous's shirts: baseball team logos, football team logos, rugby team logos. Even a few cricket teams . . . actually, no . . . he might like cricket.

THE YOU'RE GOING TO HELL APPROACH

❶ *The Walk-In Closet:* Lock Mr. Sexually Ambiguous in the closet and ask him when he wants to "come out." This doesn't really serve any purpose, but it sure is funny, right?

2. *The Strip Search:* Hire a female stripper for Mr. Sexually Ambiguous's surprise birthday party. Because there is a crowd watching . . . a crowd that expects him to act like a man . . . your boyfriend will be forced to take his eyes off the bus boy and react to those silicone breast implants and eight-inch spike-heeled boots as any self-respecting man would—like a drooling, brainless idiot.

3. *La Cosa Nostra:* Approach the local Mafia boss in your neighborhood and tell him that your boyfriend has been aching to get into "the business." Volunteer Mr. Sexually Ambiguous up as the Don's new foot soldier. The first time he tries to whack someone with two chopsticks and a potholder, he'll have to deal with Johnny "the Nut Cracker" Ravioli.

• TOP THREE GIFTS TO GIVE MR. SEXUALLY AMBIGUOUS •

1. The 2007 *Sports Illustrated* swimsuit calendar.

2. Season tickets for the NHL.

3. A pair of golf balls with a note attached that reads, "You need these more than I do".

CHAPTER 7

Stank Breath Boy

(Latin: *Chronicus halitosius*)

• OBSERVED BEHAVIOR IN NATURAL HABITAT •

While perfect in almost every way, this creature suffers from breath so vile, so lethal, so deadly to the human nostrils that you need a gas mask just to get through a conversation with him. The noxious fumes emanating from his mouth could take down a horse. His breath stinks in the morning, stinks in the afternoon, and stinks at night. There is absolutely nothing "sweet" about him whispering sweet nothings in your ear (unless you have a belt sander handy). And to make matters worse, this guy consistently scoffs at the gum you offer and the mints you place on his pillow, leaving you, and the general public, victim to his death breath.

• OFTEN HEARD SAYING •

"No thanks, I don't like mints."

"I really want to kiss you."

"Honey, why are you wearing the gas mask?

"I don't believe in going to the dentist."

"Pew! What's that smell?"

• WHY YOU MUST TAKE ACTION •

Just so you know, it is not normal for your friends to arrive at your dinner parties wearing gas masks. And again, it is not normal that your boss instituted a "no boyfriends allowed" policy at the annual office picnic for fear of your boy and his rotting mouth showing up. How many romantic ski trips to Vermont are you going to let Stank Breath Boy ruin? How much longer can you hold your breath while making love? Yes, the stench originating from this creature's boca (that's Spanish for "mouth" . . . or is it Czechoslovakian for "dentist"?) is hurting your social life and your health. You must protect yourself and the environment, for simply standing within two feet of Stank Breath Boy's oral cavity at any given time increases your chances of suffocating. If you don't fix Stank Breath Boy's chronic halitosis immediately, your otherwise perfect romance will be ruined with a single breath. Loving someone shouldn't result in respiratory failure. You cannot say "I do" until this stinker says, "I did Listerine."

• IT'S REVENGE TIME! •

In order to transform Stank Breath Boy into Fresh Breath Boy, you must do everything in your power to clean his mouth . . . or at the very least, just close it!

THE SUBTLE APPROACH

1. *The Cavity Search:* Pay off Stank Breath Boy's dentist to mail those "You're due for a checkup" reminder cards to him once a week. The more teeth cleanings he gets, the greater chance his mouth bacteria will get washed away. Not to mention the free toothbrushes he can bring home for you.

2. *One + Two = Tree:* Go to your local car wash and buy two pine tree–scented air fresheners, Dangle them from your ears so that they can be easily mistaken for earrings. Whenever Stank

Breath Boy comes within speaking distance of you, swing your head back and forth to get the fresh smell of artificial trees blowing around your nasal passages. You can't smell his bad breath through that forest!

❸ *It's Parsley for the Course:* Scientific studies show that parsley neutralizes bad breath. So from now on, every meal you cook for Stank Breath Boy should be laced with finely chopped parsley. Serve Lucky Charms with parsley milk for breakfast. Peanut butter and jelly and parsley sandwiches for lunch. Rigatoni Bolognese with parsley for dinner. Heck, toss in chocolate cupcakes with vanilla icing and parsley sprinkles for dessert!

THE NOT-SO-SUBTLE APPROACH

❶ *Mourning Breath:* According to those disgusting health specials on television, the tongue is a breeding ground for bacteria. So while the Stank Breath Boy is slumbering in the dead of night, straddle him around the ribcage area and pull his tongue out of his mouth with a pair of kitchen tongs. Then scrape all the bacteria off his tongue with a spatula.

❷ *Lemon-Aid:* Whenever Stank Breath Boy is exuding particularly noxious fumes, turn up the heat in the house and add lots of salt to whatever meal you are preparing. This will cause Stank Breath Boy to dehydrate severely. That's when you so generously offer to get him a beverage. Slip half a cup of Listerine into his lemonade.

❸ *Garlickity Split!* Rub garlic all over your body—in your hair, under your arms, under your nose. The worse you smell, the better he will.

THE YOU'RE GOING TO HELL APPROACH

1 *The Breathalyzer Test:* Being an alcoholic may land you in jail for a DUI, but it is a wonderful cure for chronic halitosis. So you are going to do whatever it takes to turn the Stank Breath Boy into a raging alcoholic. A shot of moonshine straight from the Smoky Mountains in his breakfast cereal every morning will mask that stinky breath of his faster than you can say, "I'll have another . . ." Yes, Stank Breath Boy's drinking may cost him his job and land him in AA, but at least you'll be able to stand the car ride with him to the unemployment office. (Just make sure you do the driving.)

2 *Sew What?* Sew Stank Breath Boy's mouth shut while he is sleeping. This has two benefits: (1) you won't have to smell his breath because he can't open his mouth and (2) he can never win an argument with you.

3 *A Germ of Truth:* Wear a gas mask at all times. When out to dinner. In bed. While skiing in the Bavarian Alps. Stank Breath Boy will assume you just have an irrational fear of germs. But you'll know better . . . and live longer.

• TOP THREE GIFTS TO GIVE STANK BREATH BOY •

1 Tic Tacs.

2 A pack of gum.

3 A tongue condom.

CHAPTER 8

The Can't Commit Guy

(Latin: *Engagement ringus phobias*)

● OBSERVED BEHAVIOR IN NATURAL HABITAT ●

This creature flees at the very sight of a bridal magazine, and slips into violent convulsions if you dare to suggest leaving an extra pair of socks at his place, let alone invite him to meet your parents. He freaks out if you use him as a reference on a job application or carry a photo of him in your wallet. And as far as his buddies know, you are just "a pal."

● OFTEN HEARD SAYING ●

"I can only stay for half the movie."

"Why is my name on your speed dial?"

"Dinner with your family? Uh, um . . . I'm busy."

"I hate weddings."

"I need my space."

● WHY YOU MUST TAKE ACTION ●

Despite those Botox injections you got at the grocery store, free with the purchase of a box of Cheerios, the truth of the matter is you are not getting any younger. And every day you spend with the Can't Commit Guy is a day you are wasting your love on someone who will only leave you high and dry one day. But rather than shopping for a whole new Can't Commit Guy, why not just turn this model into the *Can* Commit Guy. It's easier than you think.

• IT'S REVENGE TIME! •

The Can't Commit Guy spends his life attached to nothing and no one. You're going to change all of that in one fell swoop. And have a heck of a lot of fun doing it!

THE SUBTLE APPROACH

1. *Music to Your Ears:* Sign the Can't Commit Guy up for a life-long membership to the Columbia House CD Club. They will never let him go. EVER!

2. *Make Your Move:* Slowly but surely, leave little things of yours behind in his home. Your deodorant. Your toothbrush. Some tampons, maybe. Anything that will serve as a constant re-minder of you. And, as an added bonus, you'll have more stor-age space at *your* home!

3. *Something's Fishy Here:* Secretly add your name to all of the Can't Commit Guy's magazine subscriptions. Every time one of his periodicals arrives in the mail, he'll fall into fits of apoplexia when he sees your names linked in print.

THE NOT-SO-SUBTLE APPROACH

1. *Engaging Conversation:* Whenever you two are at a social func-tion together, introduce the Can't Commit Guy as your fiancé. Once that cat is out of the bag, there is really no going back for the poor boy.

❷ *An Inkling Here and There:* Sneeze, cough, and spit all over the Can't Commit Guy during flu season until he catches some strain of something. While playing sexy nursemaid, give him one too many capfuls of Nyquil and wait until he is delirious. Then take him to the nearest tattoo parlor, shove him in the chair, and pay Tiny to ink a giant tattoo across his forehead of a big heart with your name spelled out in it . . . followed by the word "forever."

❸ *What You Sea Is What You Get:* Book the two of you on a year-long cruise at sea. Then toss the rest of the passengers overboard so you two can have "some alone time."

THE YOU'RE GOING TO HELL APPROACH

❶ *Cuff Links:* Suggest a game of Cops and Robbers in the bedroom. Then handcuff the Can't Commit Guy not to the bedpost, but to you.

❷ *Here Comes the Bride:* Put on the biggest, poofiest wedding gown you can afford, complete with sequined veil and twenty-foot train, then wait for him to come home from work. Have a recording of "Here Comes the Bride" blaring through the stereo speakers as well. When he walks in the door, toss the bouquet in the air and squeal, "I do! I do!"

❸ *Ar-Son and His Future Daughter-in-Law:* Find out where the Can't Commit Guy's mother lives and go there without his knowledge. Make sure she is home. This is very important. When no one is looking, set fire to her house. Then, just as the fire engines arrive, bust through the front door and save his screaming mother from the flames of death. Drag her out onto the front lawn, in perfect view of all the television news cameras (which happen to be there because you called in the hot news tip right after you dialed 9–1–1). Voilà! Your are now a local hero, and his mother is indebted to you for saving her life. Makes it pretty darn tough for the Can't Commit Guy to dump you in good conscience, now doesn't it? Here comes the bride!

• TOP THREE GIFTS TO GIVE THE CAN'T COMMIT GUY •

1 His & Hers monogrammed towels.

2 A lifetime spa coupon for couples massages.

3 A leash.

CHAPTER 9

Smart Girl Tricks of the Trade

How to Get Even by Getting Over

As rock legend Pat Benatar once crooned, "Love is a battlefield." Of course, when she belted out those words, they sounded really cool; when you sing them in the shower, your neighbors just call the police. But the message still runs as deep no matter how much you butcher the melody.

For the Smart Girl surviving romance, Hell is simply a matter of being prepared for disaster at all times, and making the most of what she has. Even if it ain't much.

• HOW TO GET RID OF MR. WRONG •

Sometimes, no matter how hard the Smart Girl works at fixing up her guy, he still turns out to be Mr. Wrong. If after all of your hard work, you still haven't been able to whip your guy into shape, it is probably time to kick him to the curb. But dumping a guy is not only hard on the soul, but terrible for the complexion. So, you are going to do the smart thing, girl. Get Mr. Wrong to dump *you*. This not only enables you to avoid being forever labeled "the bitch who broke his heart," but it also gives you a chance to milk the whole "Woe is me, I got dumped" sympathy thing for at least three months. During this period of time your mother will stop nagging you, your boss will give you an extension on your project deadlines, and your friends will let you borrow even their most expensive designer shoes because they're too afraid you'll kill yourself if they don't.

But most important, by following these simple instructions, you can make room for a newer, cuter Mr. May Be Right.

1 *Monday Night Footbawl:* There is nothing that Mr. Wrong loathes more than having his spectator sports routine interrupted by one of your wailing, whiney, blubbering ball of fatty tissue girlfriends. So invite your most emotionally unstable gal pal over during Monday Night Football. Seat her next to Mr. Wrong on the couch and then sympathetically prod her to tell him, from the very beginning, the loooooooong story of exactly how she and her cat first became acquainted, and what intestinal malfunction it is presently dying from. Do this every Monday Night. Oh, and on Superbowl Sunday for sure!

2 *Please Pass the Assault:* Wait till Mr. Wrong comes home from a particularly traumatic day at work, and assail him for not having put his dirty laundry in the hamper. Then yell at him for not making the bed and forgetting that tonight is the anniversary of the first time you two kissed in front of a pigeon on a Wednesday afternoon during Daylight Savings time. Once you're finished with that, go into the bathroom and point to the poop streak on the bottom of the toilet bowl and yell at him for that, too. Then toss out his stack of car magazines and his human tooth collection. Do this three times a week until he flees the country.

3 *Driving Miss Crazy:* Whenever you two take a road trip insist on driving the car . . . and parallel parking it. Badly.

4 *Mi Casa Es Mi Mama's Casa:* Nothing will seal the fate of your love affair with Mr. Wrong faster than inviting your mother to live with you FOREVER.

5 *Live Free or Diet:* They say the way to a man's heart is through his stomach. So, let's give Mr. Wrong a bit of indigestion, shall we? If he's a meat eater, place him on a strict diet of vegetables. If he's a vegetarian, dump a tasty assortment of dead animal carcasses on his dinner plate each night. Remove all his favorite snacks from the cupboards, and replace his favorite beer with soy milk. That'll go over real well at his next Superbowl party, don't you think? Guys just love watching pro ball while sipping organic yogurt smoothies.

• DAMAGE CONTROL: CLOSE ENCOUNTERS OF THE EX KIND •

HOW TO BUMP INTO AN EX

Murphy's Law states that you will bump into your ex-boyfriend—the one who stomped on your heart and left you for dead—when and only when you have just been dumped by your rebound guy, gotten fired from your job, contracted leprosy, or are being handcuffed by the fuzz for shoplifting a papaya.

But thanks to the following Smart Girl tactics, you will always be prepared for a close encounter of the ex kind.

1 *The "Oh, I'm Not Single" Bump:* While Mr. Ex is in the midst of bragging about how wonderful his life is since he deserted you, slip your hand into your purse and press the "up" volume button on your cell phone. Doing so makes your phone sound as though it is ringing. Feign embarrassment for the intrusion, then answer your imaginary phone call from your very successful, very handsome, and very devoted imaginary boyfriend. "Oh, hi honey. I just bumped into an old friend. Yes, of course, I'm all packed for our three-week cruise to the Caribbean, silly! Just send the limo to pick me up in an hour . . ." Then say, "I love you" about fourteen times into the phone before hanging up on your imaginary boyfriend. That'll show him who is living the high life. Just make sure you pay your cell phone bill . . . that isn't imaginary.

② *The "Oh, I Don't Usually Look This Bad" Bump:* Encountering Mr. Ex when you are sans makeup and wearing your hair in a greasy bun is not the most promising way to make him regret ever leaving you. But once Mr. Ex hears that you are working undercover for the CIA as a homeless person for a "top secret government operation," he'll find even that sleep crust in the corners of your eyes sexy.

③ *The "Wow, You Got Fat!" Bump:* Remark with wide-eyed astonishment that you almost didn't recognize your ex with "all the weight" he's put on. Oh, and while you are at it mention that his forehead looks larger.

④ *Not for the Faint of Heart:* As Mr. Ex bores you with the details of his impending wedding to that Swedish supermodel, flutter your eyes, roll your head around counterclockwise, and then fall to the ground. If you're lucky, he'll give you mouth-to-mouth CPR to revive you . . . and that can easily be turned into mouth-to-tongue action.

⑤ *The Queen of Denial:* Simply refuse to admit that you are who Mr. Ex says you are and walk away. Washed up former child stars have to do it all the time.

TOP FIVE WAYS TO GET RID OF A STALKER

① Hang out in really boring places like the local library, a homeless shelter, on a park bench feeding pigeons crumbs of stale bread.

② Move next door to a police station.

③ Post a photograph of the Stalker all around town with a caption that reads, "World's Smallest Penis." He won't want to be anywhere around you or those posters lest someone recognize him.

④ Pick your nose. Even the most desperate of delinquents will be turned off by the sight of you digging for gold with your index finger shoved up your nostril for all to see.

⑤ Hit on him. The Stalker thrives on the challenge of attempting to get what he cannot have. Ask him out on a date, and his interest in you will dissipate before you can say, "Call the Police!"

MAKING USE OF BAD BOYFRIEND GIFTS

Bless their little hearts, boyfriends have the best intentions when shopping for the perfect gift for you. Yet, they always seem to make a mess of things. But fear not. Even the most thoughtless of bad boyfriend gifts serves an alternate purpose for the Smart Girl.

1. *The Oh-So-Practical Car Windshield Ice Scraper:* While you have no intention of using this thing to remove ice from your windshield (because that's something Mr. Boyfriend can do while you wait in the warm car), this thing is the perfect tool for scraping dead skin off the bottom of your feet.

2. *The Stinky Perfume:* It's not Mr. Boyfriend's fault that he bought you what amounts to an overpriced bottle of room deodorizer. Use the stinky perfume to ward off attacks from muggers. One spritz of that crap in the face, and even the most aggressive of crooks will keep running.

3. *The Cheap Vibrator:* While Mr. Boyfriend's intentions were good, he tried to save money by purchasing you the chintzy vibrator instead of the one you *really* wanted touting all the fancy bells and whistles. But you can use an unwanted vibrator gift in the kitchen when you can't find the electric mixer. Making a cake has never been quite so satisfying!

• SMART GIRL SEX •

MULTITASKING WHILE DOIN' THE NASTY

Sex is all well and good, and if you're getting some on a regular basis, more power to you. But the Smart Girl is a master of time management, and thereby multitasks while copulating. She makes the most of her time by accomplishing more than just an orgasm during sex. Every position serves an extra purpose . . . except for the one that involves hanging from the ceiling with mountain climbing clips . . . you're on your own with that, dear.

❶ *Missionary Style:* While extremely boring by today's standards, this position allows you to do important things like sort your finances since it frees up both your hands and feet. Wrap your arms around the back of Mr. Boyfriend, whisper "Oh, yes, yes, yes!" in his ear, and then, while he is pumping away, balance your checkbook over his shoulders or knit baby booties for your sister's newborn. Or dust the chandelier with your feet, if you have time . . . which is doubtful considering his record.

❷ *Doggy Style:* Being down on all fours puts you in the perfect position to catch up on some "pleasure" reading. Just slip a book in between your hands and turn the pages with your tongue. Insert the occasional "Oh yes, Baby, that feels so good" and he'll have no idea it is John Grisham you are enjoying so much.

❸ *Woman on Top:* Install a mirror on the wall above the headboard directly opposite the television in your bedroom. Climb on top of Mr. Boyfriend and face the headboard with the television remote secreted under your armpit. Mr. Boyfriend will be too busy watching your boobies jiggle up and down to notice you are watching the Home Shopping Network. When you get bored just let out a moan, and squeeze your armpit to change the channel.

"HEY BABY"— TOP FIVE RESPONSES TO CHEESY PICKUP LINES

CHEESY PICKUP LINE #1
"Excuse me, but are your feet tired? Cuz you've been running through my mind all night."

THE SMART GIRL'S RESPONSE
"Yes, they are tired, but not too tired to kick you in the nuts and halt any chances you have of procreating."

CHEESY PICKUP LINE #2
"Come here often?"

THE SMART GIRL'S RESPONSE
"Yes, but that's thanks to my vibrator, not you, pal."

CHEESY PICKUP LINE #3
"Mind if I take this seat?"

THE SMART GIRL'S RESPONSE
"Not if you're going to shove it up your ass."

④ *In the Shower:* Sex in the shower with Mr. Boyfriend is the perfect time to make sure your bathtub sparkles like new. While he's busy pumping away, grab that bottle of tile cleanser and a sponge, and make some headway with that mold. The occasional "That's right, you big hunk of love, you. You know you want it!" and he'll be none the wiser! Might be an opportune time to clean the hair out of the drain and deep-condition your hair too, eh?

⑤ *Phone Sex:* Naturally, this is the best position for the multitasking Smart Girl as it involves no physical contact whatsoever. With the help of a 2.4 mhz cordless phone, a few dirty words, and some choice panting performances, you will not only be able to satisfy the needs of your lover, but accomplish tasks you've been unable to get to. Like putting together that Fleugenboogen shelf you bought at IKEA three years ago. Writing those thank-you cards. Painting the dining room walls. Color coordinating your bras.

> **CHEESY PICKUP LINE #4**
> "You have the most beautiful eyes."
>
> **THE SMART GIRL'S RESPONSE**
> "All the better to see that I want nothing to do with you."
>
> **CHEESY PICKUP LINE #5**
> "What do you say we go back to my place and get to know each other?"
>
> **THE SMART GIRL'S RESPONSE**
> "Is that before or after you have to wash your mother's feet?"

• THE SMART GIRL LOVE COMMANDMENTS •

① *Never Go to Bed Angry:* Unless Mr. Boyfriend has cheated on you, set your parents' house on fire, or put your dog up for adoption, chances are whatever you're mad at him for doing really wasn't so bad. He may have failed to do the dishes yet again or stunk up the bathroom right before the dinner guests arrived. But are such typical male fallibilities worth spending a night on opposite sides of the bed when you two could be cuddling? No.

By all means yell at him. Heck, make him buy you some flowers. But then, Smart Girl, just let it go. Save your wrath for when Mr. Boyfriend messes up big time . . . and you know he will!

2. *Don't Keep It in When You Can Let It Out:* Confucius once said, "A couple that farts together, stays together." (Only he said it in Chinese.) In a world replete with fatty food diets and bubbly beverages there are just so many sneaky exits you can make, just so many toots you can cover up with a cough, and just so many squeaks you can mask with a sneeze before all stink points to you. You may be a pretty little thing, but you smell just as bad as he does. So, give your relationship the ultimate test and fart in his general direction. Release your gas! Show him you are woman enough to do what men do so well! We're pretty sure Mr. Boyfriend and his colon will thank you for it. Just buy some Lysol first.

3. *Just Say No:* Most women have, from time to time, made love to Mr. Boyfriend even when they weren't in the mood. (Most women reading this book have also probably peed in the shower, but we digress.) While it is understandable that you think engaging in coitus simply to please your partner is noble, lovemaking should never be a chore. The moment it becomes such, your relationship will suffer. Make love only when you both want to. Play Scrabble when you don't.

> **"IT'S NOT YOU; IT'S ME": TOP FIVE MOST RIDICULOUS BREAKUP LINES**
>
> ① "You deserve better than me."
> ② "I just need to focus on my career right now."
> ③ "I love you too much to be with you."
> ④ "This hurts me more than it hurts you."
> ⑤ "Let's be friends."

4. *The Little Things:* The simplest of indulgences can make that bitter pill called life all the more easy to swallow. Make it a practice to surprise each other with a small treat once a week. Be it

a favorite pastry, a nice back rub, or a new game to add to the PlayStation collection, small gestures of affection will keep things fresh and exciting.

5. *Respect the Mother, Even If It Hurts:* No matter how rude, obnoxious, nosey, or stupid she may be, any bad-mouthing of the mother is off limits. The bond between beastly future mother-in-law and son is unbreakable. Attacking the mother is like insulting his favorite football team. A major no-no. Keep your jokes about her cooking and that wart on her nose to yourself. Or save them for Girls Night Out.

PART TWO

The Office

"*You've Got a Staff Infection*"

• • •

Ten Signs You're a Pushover in the Office

1. You cry on your way to work each morning.

2. You use up all your sick days in the first month of the year.

3. Your job involves wearing a pirate hat and standing over a grease fryer.

4. You agree to be the coat-check girl at the office holiday parties.

5. You haven't asked for a raise since the Clinton administration.

6. You offer to work on holidays so everyone else can stay home.

7. You watch people steal your lunch from the office refrigerator and never say a word.

8. You envy unemployed people.

9. You let the coworker with the contagious flu use your phone.

10. Your picture hangs on the Worst Employee of the Month wall.

Ever wonder why your eyes tear and your stomach cramps into knots when the alarm goes off each morning? Why all the muscles in your shoulders tense up and your throat suddenly feels like you swallowed a glob of cotton? You, dear friend, are suffering from an office staff infection.

Some people love their jobs. They skip to work each morning, attend every office party with giddy enthusiasm, and cry when they leave for vacation because they'll miss everyone so much.

Unfortunately, you are not one of these people. You would rather watch an eighteen-hour documentary on the mating rituals of the tsetse fly than spend one more minute with your miserable coworkers, doing miserable work for that miserable salary. You have seen too many promotions go to unworthy coworkers, or allowed too many colleagues to take credit for your work. And if you have to listen to one more cubicle neighbor discuss the intimate details of her yeast infection with her gynecologist on company time, you are going to scream.

But quitting isn't an option, because there are bills to be paid and designer shoes to be bought. So, instead, you must build up your immune system before this job endangers your health. You must fight back against the bacteria-ridden coworkers who make your work life so hazardous. Believe it or not you have the power to cure yourself of the "staff infection" from which you are suffering. All you need is a dose of Smart Girl revenge to let the healing begin.

Now, let's meet your coworkers, shall we?

CHAPTER 10

The Office Pet

(Latin: *Kisser-us of the ass-us*)

• OBSERVED BEHAVIOR IN NATURAL HABITAT •

This creature can be found bouncing around the office with a perpetual smile on her annoying little rat face. Her photo conveniently hangs on the Employee of the Month wall every month despite the fact she does little to no work. She never gets in trouble for coming late to work or leaving early, and has a bottomless vat of "sick" days at her disposal. And although she demonstrates the intelligence of a fruit fly and the loyalty of Benedict Arnold, she inevitably gets the biggest raise, the fattest bonus, and, perhaps most irksome, the office chair with the built-in cup holders.

• OFTEN HEARD SAYING •

"Wow! Look at this great gift the boss just gave me!"

"Gee, am I the only one with the corporate credit card?"

"The boss says I'm too pretty to have to work today."

"I'm spending Christmas with the boss's family."

"Oh, I'm sorry. I can't do that. I'm busy looking through this magazine."

• WHY YOU MUST TAKE ACTION •

As long as the Office Pet is the Office Pet . . . you are NOT the Office Pet. Capice? Until you displace this brown-nosing sycophant, everything you want—every holiday bonus, every promotion, every complimentary subscription to the Sausage of the Month club—will continue to fall in her lap. Simply because she has charmed Mr. Boss. Don't let the Office Pet and her batting eyelashes stand between you and all you have worked so hard for. Knock her down a few rungs on the corporate ladder of success she's been climbing.

• IT'S REVENGE TIME! •

The Office Pet appears to have the perfect life. However, underneath that "I have it better than you" snicker is a layer of pure vulnerability on which you must pounce—pronto! (That's Italian for "fast" . . . or is it Mandarin for "onion"?) Crush this creature's ego into a pulp and exploit her weaknesses. It's time to put this annoying Pet to sleep once and for all.

THE SUBTLE APPROACH

1. *Unparallel Parking:* Around midnight on a Friday night sneak onto the office parking lot and repaint the lines on the Office Pet's Employee of the Month parking space. Narrow the width of the space by two feet, and the length by one foot. Subtle enough so that the Office Pet won't notice the change, but dramatic enough so that it will have her company-paid SUV sticking out on all sides. There are just so many fender benders Mr. Boss will tolerate before that company car gets taken back.

2. *The Nipple Effect:* Keep the office air conditioner set at precisely 61 degrees Fahrenheit. Just warm enough to keep you from developing frost bite, and just cold enough to make the Office Pet's nipples go berserk. She'll give a whole new meaning to the term "perky." She'll be so busy trying to combat her bodily functions, she won't have time to kiss ass.

3 *Wanna Be My Best Friend?* A wise man once said, "Keep your friends close, and your enemies closer." And that's exactly what you are going to do. Cozy on up to the Office Pet. Take her out to dinner once a month. Buy her extravagant gifts. Anything you have to do to forge a friendship. Then, when you two have become so sympatico that you're on the same menstrual cycle, drop the hint. "Wow, I could really use a raise . . ." Before you know it the Office Pet will be marching into the big, bad wolf's office pleading on your behalf. That means a Lamborghini isn't far behind . . . or at the very least a new roll of Scotch tape.

THE NOT-SO-NICE APPROACH

1 *His and Herpes:* According to the U.S. Board of Health one in four persons will contract a sexually transmitted disease in his or her lifetime. That means you stand a 25 percent chance of being correct when you send out a memo to the staff announcing that the Office Pet has crusty warts on her hoo-ha. Of course, it is also possible that the Office Pet is clean as a whistle and will toss herself out of the window during lunch because you have ruined her life. But hey, there's only a 75 percent chance of that happening . . .

2 *Press "Control," "Alt," "Delete":* Wipe out the Office Pet's computer hard drive—everything from her work files and e-mails to that folder called, "Work" that is, in fact, a personal file filled with guacamole recipes. Then, about a week later, when the Office Pet has been demoted to Office Putz for failure to do work in a timely fashion, swoop in and magically retrieve all her missing files. Make sure to do this while Mr. Boss is watching. Not only will the Office Pet be forever indebted to you for saving her butt; but Mr. Boss will gain a newfound admiration for your technological abilities. (Especially when you remind him of them every day via memos, e-mails, and sky writing from a small plane.)

③ *I'll Take a Bowel, Please:* Pick up a chocolate cake mix from your local grocery store and stir it in a cup with some oil and egg in the office kitchen. Then smooth the concoction on the seat of the Office Pet's chair when she isn't looking. When she sits down, she will unknowingly create a large, most offensive stain on the back of her skirt. And thus, the Office Pet becomes the Office Poop! Even the most gullible of bosses cannot bring himself to favor an employee who defecates on herself. It's bad for business.

THE YOU'RE GOING TO HELL APPROACH

① *The Missing Memo:* Intercept any and all of Mr. Boss's correspondence with the Office Pet. Tear up his memos before she reads them. Delete his e-mails from her in-box before she gets to work in the morning. Soon the Office Pet will be making such a mess of Mr. Boss's schedule that she'll be spending her lunch hour sifting through the Want Ads.

② *The Whistle-Blower:* Inform Mr. Boss that you have reason to believe the Office Pet is embezzling from the company. Present documented "proof" (a Post-it with the words, "I am embezzling from the company" will suffice). True, chances are the FBI won't find the Office Pet guilty of anything worse than pocketing some paper clips. But still, the seeds of doubt will forever be planted in Mr. Boss's tiny, tiny mind. Never again will he leave his BlackBerry out on the desk or trust the Office Pet with his credit card.

③ *While You Were Out:* Leave fake "While You Were Out" messages on Mr. Boss's desk. Write things like, "Your doctor called. He can perform the penile enlargement next Tuesday" and "That little boy you purchased on the Internet is being shipped via UPS. Should arrive tomorrow in the a.m." Then sign them all with the Office Pet's initials.

• TOP THREE GIFTS TO GIVE THE OFFICE PET •

1 Groucho Marx novelty glasses with the nose painted brown.

2 A photograph of you giving her the finger.

3 Admission tickets to the local petting zoo.

CHAPTER 11

The Office Gossip

(Latin: Flapperus of the tongue-us)

• OBSERVED BEHAVIOR IN NATURAL HABITAT •

This creature maneuvers around the office like a fox stalking prey, licking her salivating chops at the mere thought of sinking her teeth into a gossipy tidbit. She roams the office landscape in search of scandal, eyes constantly darting from left to right, ears perched in a permanent state of alert. And when she finally does come upon a matter of intrigue that is, of course, none of her business whatsoever, she pounces on it, embellishes upon it, and then disseminates the news with lightning speed to other interested parties via the phone, the Internet, or a low-level whisper.

• OFTEN HEARD SAYING •

"You didn't hear this from me, but . . ."

"I don't like talking about people behind their backs, but . . ."

"You're never gonna believe what I just heard!"

"Pssssssst."

"Yes, of course I can keep a secret . . ."

• WHY YOU MUST TAKE ACTION •

The Office Gossip and her non-stop mouth have been making your life a living Hell since Day One. She is the reason everyone knows you got a yeast infection from wearing your wet bathing suit too long at the office pool party. And that you had a one-night stand with the air conditioning repair guy. Nothing you say or do is safe around this girl.

How much longer is she going to be allowed to eavesdrop on your personal phone calls? Or inform Human Resources that you are "with child" when, in fact, you simply ate one too many tacos the night before? You and your yeast infection have a constitutional right to privacy! If you don't shut this motormouth up, everything you do and say, and even some things you don't do or say, will become fodder for your coworkers.

• IT'S REVENGE TIME! •

Gossiping is only fun when you're the one doing it. So, let's get started! It is time for you to silence the Office Gossip once and for all.

THE SUBTLE APPROACH

1. *Can You Repeat That, Please?* Any time you catch the Office Gossip whispering in someone's ear about you, shout out the following across the office, "I'm sorry. Can you speak up? I can't hear what you're saying about me from over here!" Then smile widely and toss in a casual wave. Gossiping is very hard to do when one keeps getting interrupted, by the subject of the gossip, no less.

2. *Heavy Meddle Phone:* Whenever you must make a personal phone call in the office, turn up the speakers on your computer and blast a music CD. Metallica or AC/DC works particularly well in such instances. The sound of raging guitar riffs and screeching vocals about death will make it impossible for the Office Gossip to hear anything you are saying. And that, dear friend, gives her nothing to talk about. Problem solved!

③ *Message to the Masses # 1:* Change the Office Gossip's outgoing voice mail recording to "Hi, I'm sorry I can't take your call right now. Please leave a message, but be aware anything you say may be repeated by me to other interested parties."

THE NOT-SO-SUBTLE APPROACH

❶ *Lipschtick:* When she's not looking, sneak into the Office Gossip's cosmetic bag and apply a few drops of industrial-strength glue to the tip of her lipstick. When she goes to touch up her makeup on her bathroom break, this blabber mouth will find her lips permanently sealed. The only gossip she'll be able to spread is "Mmmmmmmmmm." And who wants to listen to that?

❷ *A Sign of the Times:* Begin communicating at the office via sign language. This will make it next to impossible for the Office Gossip to eavesdrop on any of your water cooler chat with coworkers.

❸ *Message to the Masses # 2:* Change the Office Gossip's outgoing voice mail recording to "Hi, I'm sorry I can't take your call right now. I'm too busy telling lies about people in the office because I am terribly insecure."

THE YOU'RE GOING TO HELL APPROACH

❶ *What Goes Around, Comes Around:* Spread a rumor around the office that the Office Gossip is being fired. This will circulate extremely quickly and make it back to her in no time. And no matter how much Mr. Boss denies the rumor when confronted by the Office Gossip, the seeds of doubt will already be planted in that pea brain of hers.

❷ *Heard It Through the Grapevine:* "Hey, [insert Office Gossip's name here] just told me that you are suffering from erectile dysfunction. I just wanted to express my deepest sympathies to you and the Mrs."

❸ *Message to the Masses # 3:* Change the Office Gossip's outgoing voice mail recording to "I'm sorry I can't take your call right now. I am presently suffering from a vicious herpes outbreak and must get some genital warts burned off at my gynecologist's office right away. Please leave a message."

• TOP THREE GIFTS TO GIVE THE OFFICE GOSSIP •

❶ A muzzle.

❷ A book on karma.

❸ A list of people who hate her.

CHAPTER 12

Little Miss Sunshine

(Latin: *Donna Reedus*)

• OBSERVED BEHAVIOR IN NATURAL HABITAT •

This creature is inevitably a blonde with pearly white teeth and a speaking voice so high-pitched, dolphins hear it from two continents away. Her outfits are always adorned with "Smile! It's a New Day!" and "Do You Need a Hug?" buttons, and she skips to work each morning. Her spare time is spent doing annoyingly humane things like sponsoring canned-food drives and volunteering for the Peace Corps. Bo-o-o-ring!

• OFTEN HEARD SAYING •

"Turn that frown upside down."

"If life hands you lemons, make lemonade!"

"Have a great day and make all your dreams come true!"

"Don't you just love life?!"

"I'm spending my vacation working in Guam with underprivileged children."

• WHY YOU MUST TAKE ACTION •

Put yourself in Mr. Boss's position for a moment. Whom would you rather promote? The bitter and angry employee who growls at her desk eight hours a day and can't get along with anyone? (You.) Or bubbly Little Miss Sunshine who believes that every problem can be solved with a hug?

Exactly.

The longer Little Miss Sunshine and her exasperating optimism flit about the office the harder it is for you to shine. So before Little Miss Sunshine gets the whole staff holding hands and singing a round of "Kumbaya," you must smack that smile off her face. After all, if every cloud has a silver lining, then every silver lining must have a cloud!

● IT'S REVENGE TIME! ●

Listen and listen carefully. Little Miss Sunshine is a fraud. No one can be that cheerful all the time. It's not human. Any freak who pastes inspirational quotes all over her bulletin board is clearly battling some demons. Expose this imposter for the depression-bound creature she truly is. The sooner Little Miss Sunshine's cover is blown, the less bitter and angry you'll look to Mr. Boss.

THE SUBTLE APPROACH

1. *The Un-Smiley Face:* With a permanent black marker turn exactly one-third of the smiley faces decorating Little Miss Sunshine's cubicle into frowns. Pencil in a black tooth in a few just for good measure.

2. *Don't Say Cheese, Please:* Leave a fake memo from Mr. Boss on Little Miss Sunshine's desk that warns of immediate suspension of any employee caught smiling. This girl is not a risk taker, and just like the rest of us, needs to pay the bill. She can't afford to take any chances, even if it means keeping those sparkling white teeth out of sight for a few hours.

3. *The Hallmark Moment:* Let all the imbeciles in the office add their cutesy "Wishing you all the best!" comments to Little Miss Sunshine's birthday card. You're going to write something much

more memorable. Like, "Happy Birthday—enjoy it because it's probably your last." Or "Are you sure that mole on your face isn't a tumor?"

THE NOT-SO-SUBTLE APPROACH

1 *Listerwrong!* Add a few drops of black food coloring to the travel bottle of Listerine Little Miss Sunshine keeps in her top drawer. When she goes to freshen her breath after lunch, she will unknowingly dye her teeth a ghoulish tint. This, in turn, will force her to avoid smiling for the rest of the day.

2 *Stickin' It to Her:* Right before Little Miss Sunshine and her equally annoying peace-lovin' friends are about to leave for Woodstock 2007, place a bumper sticker on the rear fender of her 1971 Volkswagen van that reads, "Make War, Not Peace." Who said hippies can't get violent?

3 *"Why the Long Face?"* Every time you pass by Little Miss Sunshine's desk, stop dead in your tracks, take a long look at her, and say, "Why do you look so sad?" She will inevitably argue that she is never sad, at which point you simply shake your head and reply, "Oh, sorry. My mistake. You just seem really upset about something." Nothing drives a perpetually cheerful person more insane than being mistaken for a sad person. Do this once a day until she kills herself.

THE YOU'RE GOING TO HELL APPROACH

1 *Recipe for Disaster:* For this mission, you will need the following:

- A small plastic sandwich bag
- A small food scale

- A canister of oregano
- Some confectioners sugar
- A compact mirror
- A razor blade

Arrive at the office before everyone else, and set up shop at Little Miss Sunshine's desk. Place the compact mirror on her desk and sprinkle two lines of the confectioner's sugar on top of it. Leave the razor blade in between the two lines. Fill the sandwich baggie with about two grams of the oregano and leave that in her top drawer. Toss around a few pamphlets from the local drug counseling clinic and you've just given Little Miss Sunshine a very public substance abuse problem.

2. *The Gift of Giving:* Sign Little Miss Sunshine up to be a live organ donor. She won't have much to smile about as she watches two men in white coats carry her internal organs away in a beach cooler.

3. *Die, Bitch, Die!:* Actually write "Die, Bitch! DIE!" on Little Miss Sunshine's birthday card—but sign it from another one of your office nemeses. The perfect killing of two bird brains with one stone. You'll put a frown on one's face and simultaneously stir up trouble for another. Sit back and watch Little Miss Sunshine's face cloud over with sadness as she reads the nasty sentiment, then turns to the other colleague, with whom she had drinks just two nights ago, with a look of utter confusion. Guess it wasn't such a Happy Hour after all, huh?

• TOP THREE GIFTS TO GIVE LITTLE MISS SUNSHINE •

1. *Bambi* on DVD . . . cued up to the part where Bambi's mom gets shot.

2. A photo of Mother Teresa with a caption that reads, "You can't compete."

3. The Book of the Apocalypse.

CHAPTER 13

The Hypochondriac

(Latin: *Snifflus profuseus*)

● OBSERVED BEHAVIOR IN NATURAL HABITAT ●

This creature's presence is always accompanied by a random assortment of neck braces, crutches, Band-Aids, and cold remedies. She sneezes, sniffles, coughs, or gasps her way through the workday, and is constantly coming in late or leaving early for doctor's appointments intended to cure her disease du jour. She is always on the phone with either a doctor, an insurance company, or a lawyer and single-handedly uses up more office tissues in one week than some countries dispose of in a year.

● OFTEN HEARD SAYING ●

"I think I'm allergic to this copy paper."

"I think I'm allergic to this Wite-Out."

"I think I'm allergic to this pen."

"I think I'm allergic to your perfume."

"I think I'm allergic to the air."

• WHY YOU MUST TAKE ACTION •

Ever wonder why your health insurance premiums are so high? It's because of this jackass. That's right. You're paying more and more money each year for medical coverage you barely use because nitwits like this are sucking the health care industry dry. While you're dragging your flu-infected ass into work just so you can complete the "big project" on time, the Hypochondriac calls in sick over a stubbed toe. With her abuse of sick days and visits to the doctor on company time for ailments a normal person would treat with rubbing alcohol and a Band-Aid, the Hypochondriac's antics are giving YOU an ulcer!

• IT'S REVENGE TIME! •

The Hypochondriac may have gotten out of filing those papers because of her severe allergy to staples, but you have something she doesn't: a sick mind. And a sick mind is a terrible thing to waste. Prey on this wench's allergies, phobias, and psychoses until she quarantines herself for good.

That's right, Smart Girl. You're about to give the Hypochondriac a taste of her own psychosomatic medicine . . .

THE SUBTLE APPROACH

1. *Eau de Stink:* Go to a "Dollar" store . . . you know—one of those creepy bargain places that sell no-name shampoos and car deodorizers shaped like Jesus . . . and pick up an assortment of the most odiferous bargain perfumes you can find. Preferably with a skunk-based scent. Each morning douse yourself with your Eau de Stink of the day and watch the Hypochondriac's sinuses flair! A terrific way to bring her to tears. Who knew you could have so much fun with a dollar?

2. *It's All in the Phlegmaly:* Nothing terrifies the Hypochondriac more than the spread of germs. So, hack up some bile at the copy machine, sneeze on the phones, wipe your nose, and then

touch her keyboard. Heck, puke on her desk if you have to. There isn't enough Lysol in the world to keep this girl from freaking out!

3. *You've Got Mail:* Send the Hypochondriac daily false e-mail alerts warning her about contagious diseases she can catch from performing typical work duties. Convince her that "Desks can be hazardous to your health!" and "Staplers transmit Ebola!" and "Pens give you Ebola." Eventually, she'll fall so far behind in her work Mr. Boss will have no choice but to cut her loose. With a deadly airborne disease nonetheless.

THE NOT-SO-SUBTLE APPROACH

1. *What's in a Name?* Secretly replace the Hypochondriac's Lysol with pepper spray. Then sit back and watch the wheezing, gasping, and fainting begin. A great way to kill a few hours on a slow day at work.

2. *I Can Do That!* The Hypochondriac is sorely mistaken if she thinks she has the monopoly on imaginary illnesses. Whatever disease or injury this creature acquires, you will one-up her. She comes in with a head cold? Well, you'll come down with the flu! She hops in on crutches? You'll just cut off your legs and roller derby in that new wheelchair of yours. She's suffering from a severe case of eczema? Go get yourself a case of that flesh-eating virus thing. The Hypochondriac will get so distressed watching you steal the show (and all her sick days), she'll eventually have to come in dead to top you.

3. *I'm Okay; You're Not:* Every time you walk past the Hypochondriac's desk, say any of the following things: "What's wrong with your face?" "Are you getting a fever or something?" "What's that thing on your forehead?" It won't be long before

this sickie is at the local library diagnosing herself with the latest trendy disease.

THE YOU'RE GOING TO HELL APPROACH

1 *No Assurance Without Insurance:* Were it not for the wonders of health insurance the Hypochondriac would undoubtedly end up in the poorhouse thanks to all those doctor visits and drug prescriptions. So, imagine the havoc you can wreak on her sick body and soul by canceling her medical coverage! Soon enough the Hypochondriac will be forced to suffer through a cold like the rest of us—drunk on Nyquil.

2 *The Grinch Who Stole Christmas:* The evening before the office Christmas party call the Hypochondriac at home. Inform her that the Centers for Disease Control have quarantined the entire office due to a deadly airborne virus that has been leaking through the ventilation system, and that all employees have been instructed to stay home until further notice. Then put on your best party outfit and head out to the festivities!

3 *Dial 9–1–1:* Every time the Hypochondriac lets out a mere hiccup, run around the office screaming, "OH MY GOD! She's dying! Call 9–1–1!" Have the paramedics put the Hypochondriac through all sorts of trauma, like strapping her down to a gurney and forcing tubes in her veins and shoving oxygen hoses up her nose. Travel in the ambulance with her so that she can hear when you call her next of kin to inform them of her "imminent death." When she argues that she is feeling fine, just shake your head and sigh, "Oh dear, that's one of the symptoms. Denial." Toss in a few calls to a funeral home for good measure. You can be sure it'll be a long while before the Hypochondriac coughs in public again.

• TOP THREE GIFTS TO GIVE THE HYPOCHONDRIAC •

1. A surgical mask.

2. A rectal thermometer.

3. A body condom.

CHAPTER 14

The Office Ho

(Latin: *Whoreus maximus*)

• OBSERVED BEHAVIOR IN NATURAL HABITAT •

Her "enhanced" breasts are always straining the buttons of her low-cut blouse. She's often overheard on the phone discussing her recent sexual conquests. Whenever a male staff member walks by, she bats her eyelashes and winks—then turns to you and gives you that "yeah, I did him" sneer. She uses her sex to get what she wants, and boy, does it work!

• OFTEN HEARD SAYING •

"Yep, I did him . . . and him . . . and her . . ."

"Does anyone have a condom?"

"I think I'm pregnant . . . again."

"I can put my ankles behind my ears. Can you?"

"Yes, that was me in that porno."

• WHY YOU MUST TAKE ACTION •

As your Grandma Ruthie used to say, "Heavens to Betsy! Why would a gentleman buy the cow when he can get the milk for free?"

The same theory applies when working alongside the Office Ho. With her generously donating her sexual services around the office, it is next to impossible to compete for the copy machine repair guy's attention. Not to mention the fact that her very presence in the office exposes you to all sorts of disgusting venereal diseases. But the damage she can inflict on your professional life is even worse, for the Office Ho has big boobs and a flexible tongue . . . and she knows how to use them to acquire raises, promotions, and the fancy swivel chair with the massage feature. Anything and everything for which you work so hard, the Office Ho takes away with a shake of her hips and her plunging neckline.

• IT'S REVENGE TIME! •

You may not be able to compete with her size 44DD boobies or ability to suck a golf ball through a garden hose. But fret not. There are ways to put the Office Ho in her place and still maintain your dignity.

THE SUBTLE APPROACH

1. *The Virus:* In front of everyone including Mr. Boss, point to the Office Ho and whisper, "She has a virus. We should all be careful." Then, just when things begin to get uncomfortable, point to her computer and conclude, "We should run a virus scan on her computer just to make sure everything is okay."

2. *For a Good Time, Call . . .* Go into the office men's room where the Office Ho has written her number all over the bathroom stalls and change one digit on the phone number to match that of a local eatery. This will put a serious crimp in the Office Ho's sex life, but more important, it will rock her self-confidence. Why aren't all the men calling her for a good time? Well, hee hee, you know why! They're all too busy calling Tino's Pizza Parlor!

3. *The Virgin Mary:* Sign the Office Ho up to be on the mailing list for one of those "Born Again Virgin" cults. Those people could convert Mary Magdalene!

THE NOT-SO-SUBTLE APPROACH

❶ *The Tit-Tac-Tic:* With the tip of your envelope opener spring a leak in the Office Ho's water bra during an office meeting. Get a good laugh watching her cleavage deflate from a DD to an AAA.

❷ *The Computer Scream Saver:* When the Office Ho is on her lunch break, hop onto her computer and change the settings for her screen saver. Program her desktop so it no longer showcases that adorable photograph of her puppy, but instead flashes a banner that reads: "I have chlamydia." Talk about a computer virus!

❸ *Debbie Can't Do Dallas:* Knock the Office Ho unconscious with a stapler. Then drag her body into the supply closet and strap a chastity belt onto her. This will put her out of commission for a while. Or at least until she can get her hands on some bolt cutters.

THE YOU'RE GOING TO HELL APPROACH

❶ *Hair Today, Gone Tomorrow:* Slip a few dabs of hair remover into the Office Ho's shampoo bottle which she keeps in a gym bag under her desk. Even the most horny of men would prefer a date with his left hand to having sex with a bald chick.

❷ *Dick Tracy:* Spread a rumor that the Office Ho has a penis. Any guy who *has* slept with her won't dare challenge the gossip for fear of being labeled a closet homosexual. And any guy who was *planning* on sleeping with her will most definitely find you instantly more attractive . . . even if you don't kiss on the first date!

❸ *I've Been Diaphragm-ed!* When the Office Ho isn't looking, reach into her bag and pull out whatever form of birth control she is packing. If it's the Pill, secretly switch a few of the tablets for children's aspirin. If it's the diaphragm, punch a whole in it with a ballpoint pen. Condoms? Cut the tip off. Her impending maternity leave means a few months of Heaven for you. Sure, these are really mean, but we don't call this section "You're Going to Hell" for nothin'!

• TOP THREE GIFTS TO GIVE THE OFFICE HO •

1   Clean sheets.

2   A turtleneck.

3   Cold sore medicine.

CHAPTER 15

Sticky Fingers

(Latin: *Takerus of what is not-us hersus*)

● OBSERVED BEHAVIOR IN NATURAL HABITAT ●

She rummages through your purse when you step away from your desk and thinks nothing of replacing her empty printer ink cartridge with yours when you're not looking. She has stolen food out of your bag lunches (which by the way makes you a geek) and you are pretty sure that is your watch she is wearing.

Her eyes are always shifting from left to right in search of something to filch, and she is a big fan of prison shows.

● OFTEN HEARD SAYING ●

"Sure, I'd be happy to watch your bag for you."

"That's a really nice necklace you're wearing. How much is it worth?"

"Hey, does anyone know how to deactivate the alarm system?"

"No, I don't have a criminal record."

"Damn! Is that the fuzz?"

• WHY YOU MUST TAKE ACTION •

Figure it out, Einstein. Working in close proximity to someone who is organizing *her* schedule on *your* BlackBerry is a bad, bad thing. What is the point of getting birthday gifts from loved ones if they're going to end up in Sticky Finger's possession? Why go to the trouble of buying that terrific cashmere sweater if it's gonna get stolen the next day? You work hard for your money, and deserve the right to buy nice things . . . and more important, *keep* them! Yes, your office is a place of wretched melancholy and despair. But it should also be a safe haven for your belongings. You should be able to keep your purse under your desk without fear of the cash inside going missing when you step away to make a copy. Besides, you are fairly certain that is your credit card she just used to purchase a plasma television.

• IT'S REVENGE TIME! •

Sticky Fingers may have gotten off with your cell phone and the watch your father gave you for your birthday. But the stolen buck stops here! Teach this little thief that there are consequences to her actions and some of them involve a 6-by-8 cell.

THE SUBTLE APPROACH

1. *It's All in the Label:* Cut up little pieces of paper and type, "This belongs to [insert your name here]." With industrial-strength adhesive attach said labels to every single object at your desk from the tape dispenser to the computer to your pens and stapler. Your lunch bag too, since you're apparently geek enough to bring one in. Sticky Fingers cannot chance stealing goods that have your name written all over them . . . literally.

2. *Big Brother Is Watching:* Place a large sign on the outside of your work space that reads, "This Area Is Under 24-Hour Surveillance" and mount a toy video camera in your cubicle.

Add a "Beware of Rabid Rottweiler" sign to the wall for extra effect.

❸ *Faux Riche:* If you aren't doing so already, begin wearing designer fakes of everything. Sticky Fingers will work her butt off trying to get a hold of that $3,000 watch you've been sporting only to discover its street value is about $12.50.

THE NOT-SO-SUBTLE APPROACH

❶ *The Bagged Lunch:* If Sticky Fingers is in the habit of noshing on your bag lunch (did we mention this makes you a geek?), use it to your advantage. Smother that tuna fish sandwich with past-due mayonnaise. Slip in a pesticide-soaked apple and some moldy Saltines, a few pieces of sugar-free chocolate, and cheese that dates back to Louis XIV's reign. Pretty soon your bag lunch will be as safe as can be in that fridge. (But you're still a geek for bringing it.)

❷ *Arrested Development:* Have one of your male friends dress up as a police officer and stop by your office to "investigate some recent thefts." Let him "dust for prints," take some Polaroids, and "run some DNA samples down at the lab." If Sticky Fingers has been keeping up with this season's *CSI* and knows what's good for her, she'll be afraid to steal from you ever again.

❸ *Stuck on You:* Glue everything you own to your desk. Paper clips, pens, staplers, rules, your desktop calendar. Yes, you may lose your job for failure to do your work in a timely fashion. But we really can't worry about that now, can we?

THE YOU'RE GOING TO HELL APPROACH

❶ *Carpe Dum Dum:* Everyone knows that Sticky Fingers has, well, sticky fingers. So take advantage of the deflected attention.

This is your chance to get away with all the office goodies at someone else's expense. Thinking of a fax machine for your home office? Steal it and watch Sticky Fingers take the fall. Need a new desktop for your den? Take that, too! You'll never get blamed for the thievery because everyone knows who the "real" perpetrator is.

2 *Fur Better or Worse:* Let Sticky Fingers really suffer for it when she steals that fur jacket you conveniently wore to work. Wait till she slips out of the building and into her new fur jacket. Then call PETA and tell them there is a violent animal abuser on the block.

3 *The Electric Fence:* Around the perimeter of your work space install one of those electric fences that zaps a shot of electricity through the body of any trespasser. Sticky Fingers can withstand just so many volts before she'll give up and steal from someone else. (Just make sure to deactivate the system when other people are entering . . . namely Mr. Boss.)

• TOP THREE GIFTS TO GIVE STICKY FINGERS •

1 A pair of handcuffs with her name engraved on them.

2 Mittens.

3 A photo of death row inmates awaiting execution.

CHAPTER 16

The Chauvinist Pig

(Latin: *Modernus neanderthalus*)

• OBSERVED BEHAVIOR IN NATURAL HABITAT •

This jerk spends his workday scratching his balls, ogling your breasts, mocking women's sports teams, and hanging posters of bikini-clad women straddling Corvettes all over his office. He laughs if you try to lift a pencil without assistance, and audibly scoffs at any professional success you achieve because he believes it can only be the direct result of sexual favors, not hard work. Oh, and he is usually single. *Quel surprise!*

• OFTEN HEARD SAYING •

"Let me help you with that, little lady."

"A woman's place is in the kitchen . . ."

"Nice rack."

"Wow! You can read?"

"Man, I bagged one hot babe last night."

• WHY YOU MUST TAKE ACTION •

The Chauvinist Pig is one of the most vile, despicable, and grotesque creatures on the planet. In homage to the brave women who marched for the ERA back in the '70s you must take a stand against this Neanderthal. What are you thinking letting this jerk make PMS jokes about you and imply that you slept your way to the top?! (Everyone knows you slept your way to the bottom.) This Cretan must be shoved back in his pen before you put the feminist movement back centuries. Trust us, you do NOT want a bunch of angry women in tank tops and bandanas mad at you. Some of those gals can bench-press a rhinoceros.

● IT'S REVENGE TIME!

Nothing ruins the Chauvinist Pig's day more than a woman in power. And you, Smart Girl, have the power. All you have to do is learn how to use it and abuse it. Try any one of the following tactics to take this potbellied piglet down so hard his testicles hit the ground. (And they are very, very tiny testicles, by the way.)

THE SUBTLE APPROACH

1. *The Old Switcheroo:* Every few days or so switch the sign on the men's and women's restrooms. Walking into the opposite sex's bathroom once or twice can be explained as an accident. But after the Chauvinist Pig does it for the fortieth or fiftieth time? Well, now we're looking at a reason to contact Human Resources!

2. *Bareback Mountain:* You can tell a lot about a person by his screen saver, which is precisely why you are going to change the Chauvanist Pig's screen saver from that photo of Roger Staubach posing with a football to a still shot from the homosexual cowboy romance *Brokeback Mountain.* By the time he realizes his computer is a tribute to Heath Ledger's pectoral muscles and Jake Gyllen-haal's butt, the damage has already been done.

3. *Won't You Join Us?* Sign the Chauvinist Pig up for Oprah's website e-mail alerts. There are just so many times this Neanderthal

can receive invitations to Oprah's Web forum on "America's Most Powerful Women" without giving his sexist philosophy some second thought.

THE NOT-SO-SUBTLE APPROACH

❶ *Yes Sir, Ma'am:* Keep calling him "Miss" by "accident." If you do this enough, the Chauvinist Pig will begin to wonder if it's something he's doing wrong.

❷ *Ooops! I Did It Again:* Wear a really tight skirt to work and pull the old "Whoops! Dropped my papers" bend-over trick. Wait until the Chauvinist Pig cozies right up behind you to grab your butt, and then release the stinkiest fart your bowels can muster. (Downing a can of Hormel Chili the night before is particularly helpful.)

❸ *Mr. Coffee:* In your best helpless, girlie voice, ask the Chauvinist Pig to help little ole you operate the coffee machine. This is the moment he has been waiting for! As he approaches, snickering and snorting in his usual piggy way, explode the coffee all over his shirt and tie. Then bat your eyelashes and squeal, "Oh, I'm soooo sorry! I just don't understand this modern technology." From then on the Chauvinist Pig will be torn between wanting to prove girls can't operate heavy machinery . . . and keeping his wardrobe from smelling like hazelnut mocha.

THE YOU'RE GOING TO HELL APPROACH

❶ *My, What Big Boobs You Have:* Slip small doses of estrogen into the Chauvinist Pig's coffee each morning. Slowly but surely the hormones will kick in, and before long he'll be sporting man boobs with that Armani tie.

② *Happy Birthday!:* Hire a she-male stripper for the Chauvinist Pig's birthday party. Then videotape the lap dance and broadcast it on the Internet. Send a copy to his mother, too . . . and his poker buddies . . . oh, and his preacher.

③ *Be My Bitch:* Sign the Chauvinist Pig up for a prison outreach program. Tell him Mr. Boss is giving a $10,000 bonus to any employee who spends a weekend teaching calisthenics at the local maximum security facility. Then pay one of the guards to lock him in Cell Block C for the weekend. One evening alone with Bubba and this creep will be all woman!

● TOP THREE GIFTS TO GIVE THE CHAUVINIST PIG ●

① A signed first edition copy of Gloria Steinem's biography.

② Season tickets to a professional women's basketball game.

③ A T-shirt that reads, "A Man's Place Is in the Kitchen."

CHAPTER 17

Mr. Boss

(Latin: *Powerus hungryus jerkus*)

• OBSERVED BEHAVIOR IN NATURAL HABITAT •

This creature is heard, but rarely seen, only appearing among the inferior members of the tribe to feed, yell, or whine. He wears expensive suits, but their impact is somewhat diminished by the crusty flakes of dandruff that cling to them. He drives a company car, charges every meal to the company account, and somehow convinced the IRS that his annual visits to the Pussycat Ranch in Reno are a business expense.

• OFTEN HEARD SAYING •

"You're late!"

"I need you to be more proactive."

"Has anyone seen my BlackBerry?"

"I can be reached at my beach house."

"What's your name again?"

• WHY YOU MUST TAKE ACTION •

Remember the creepy little guy behind the curtain at the end of the film, *The Wizard of Oz*? Well, think of Mr. Boss as that creepy little guy, only a bit taller and driving a Lexus. He may be pushing buttons and barking the occasional order here and there, but everyone knows that Oz is primarily fueled by the hard work of those under-appreciated Lollipop Guild-ing Munchkins. And sadly, you are one of those under-appreciated Munchkins . . . albeit slightly taller. But why should he get all the glory, while you do all the hard work, right? True, you drop 43 percent of his calls, and don't really know what you're doing most of the time. But that's besides the point. Mr. Boss has leeched off your hard work for too long, and it's high time you return the favor by beating him slowly at his own corporate game. Sabotage your way to those long overdue extended lunch breaks and extra sick days, girl! Bring Mr. Boss to his knees, and you'll be zipping on down that Yellow Brick Road in no time . . . in a company car to boot!

• IT'S REVENGE TIME! •

Beating Mr. Boss at his own game is just a matter of preying on his weaknesses and testing his patience every chance you get. The more leverage you gain, the fatter your paycheck will be!

THE SUBTLE APPROACH

1. *Pickin' on the BlackBerry # 1:* If your Mr. Boss is like most Mr. Bosses, he is entirely dependent on his BlackBerry to keep atop his busy schedule. But any fool who relies on a palm-size electronic organizer made in Taiwan by little slave children to plan his day deserves his comeuppance. Delete one or two of Mr. Boss's most important phone number contacts and the automatic reminder of his wife's birthday. Then, just when Mr. Boss is about to get his head bitten off by Mrs. Boss because he forgot her birthday, swoop in and remind him that he needs to bring home flowers. He'll be indebted to you for remembering what he forgot . . . and getting him some long overdue hanky panky in the process.

❷ *In God We Trust:* Take advantage of the fact that, by law, a supervisor cannot question, mock, or restrict an employee's religious beliefs. So, take up random religious practices each week to interfere with Mr. Boss's workday. Carry a prayer mat around the office and kneel to Mecca during board meetings. Chant passages from the Torah while on the phone with clients. Convert your cubicle into a Buddhist shrine and slap a Hindu dot on your forehead. Make your search for God Mr. Boss's personal Hell. And if he gives you trouble for ordering that living Nativity set from JesusLovesMe.com on the company's credit card? Well, point out you can always observe your religions during your lunch hour from now on . . . your *extended* lunch hour, that is.

❸ *Injured in the Line of Duty:* An injured employee is an annoying employee. Broken appendages, sprained ankles, twisted vertebrae—they all require special accommodations, which, in turn, cost the company money. And that drives Mr. Boss crazy. So fall off that chair and break your arm. Slip on the floor and sprain your neck. Go blind in one eye or deaf in one ear. The more time you spend at work hobbling around on crutches, crashing into things with your wheelchair, the better. When Mr. Boss finally blows his top because you are having an elevator installed in your cubicle, munificently suggest that none of this special treatment would be necessary if you could work from home.

THE NOT-SO-SUBTLE APPROACH

❶ *Pickin' on the BlackBerry #2:* Chances are Mr. Boss hasn't backed up his PDA for at least three months. So, secretly copy all his files onto your computer and then hit the RE-SET button on his BlackBerry to delete everything. Then, just when he is about to get in major trouble with the head office for losing that corporate donor spreadsheet, swoop in and salvage all his "lost" information. Mr. Boss will ask how he can ever repay you for

your help. That's when you hand him the *Sharper Image* cata-
log you conveniently have on hand. (Who doesn't want a foot
massager / rocket launcher / hammock?)

② *Tic Toc:* Imagine how annoyed Mr. Boss will be when you begin
walking around the office twitching your eyes inexplicably or
making inadvertent grunting noises at the copy machine. Take
on a bizarre new tic every week—a random kicking of the leg at
the fax machine, the flapping of your arms at the copier.
Anything that makes you look like you are being electrocuted.
Soon Mr. Boss will be more than happy to shorten your workday as requested . . . just to get rid of you and your annoying
body seizures.

③ *Silence Is Golden:* Inform Mr. Boss you are training to be a nun
and must observe a vow of silence in the office. (The chances
of Mr. Boss actually investigating the legitimacy of your claim
are pretty slim . . . mostly because the number for the local
nunnery was in his BlackBerry you reset.) Begin using a made
up sign language to communicate with him. Eventually, he will
find this signing crap so frustrating he'll simply bother the
Office Pet for help when he needs something done. And that
means more free time for you to spend shopping on the
Internet, missy!

THE YOU'RE GOING TO HELL APPROACH

① *An Affair to Remember . . . and Document:* At the next office
holiday party, wait until Mr. Boss is really drunk. Then shove
him into his office, strip him naked, and lay him on top of an
equally naked and voluptuous inflatable doll. Snap a few choice
pictures of Mr. Boss and the lovely, but inflatable "Peggy,"
preferably with his tongue in "Peggy's" equally inflatable ear.
Then leave said photos in a sealed envelope on his desk with a
note attached reading, "I think I need a raise, Boss, don't you?"

② *F—k You, Sir:* Secretly sneak dirty words into letters Mr. Boss has you type on his behalf. For instance, "Dear Sirs, on behalf of my small [change the word "company" for "penis"] I would like to invite you to attend my annual [change the word "picnic" to "bestiality convention"]. Of course, this will do nothing but get you in trouble. But it sure is fun!

③ *Kill, Kill, Kill:* While a bit risky and most definitely unethical, this tactic does pretty much guarantee you will never have to deal with the bastard again. Yes, there is the slight chance you will get arrested and sentenced to life in prison. But that's a chance any Smart Girl is willing to take. Simply go on the Internet and hire a professional hit man. Schedule the hit to co-incide with your vacation in Mexico so you cannot be connected with the crime. Oh, and make sure to attend the funeral and weep uncontrollably over his coffin. Some flowers to the family wouldn't kill you either . . . but charge them to Mr. Boss's corporate card. (It's not like he's gonna be needing it anymore, right?)

• TOP THREE GIFTS TO GIVE MR. BOSS •

① A watch that is off by twenty-two minutes.

② An enema kit.

③ A briefcase that doesn't open.

CHAPTER 18

Smart Girl Tricks of the Trade

How to Get Even by Getting Over

One of the best ways to get even in the workplace is not to do any work at all. After all, your day can be much better spent shopping on the Internet, making personal phone calls, and writing in your diary. A Smart Girl gets even by getting over. Just practice these simple steps and you'll be well on your way to *not* earning that paycheck!

• HOW TO USE THE INTERNET ON COMPANY TIME •

If you are fortunate enough to have access to the Internet at work, use it for your personal gain! The key is to simply not get caught doing so. Think about it: You can spend upward of eight hours a day shopping—and here's the beautiful part—get paid to do it!

1 Sit as close to your computer as is humanly possible and use the width of your torso and big, fat head to block Mr. Boss's view of your computer monitor. What he can't see, he can't yell at you for.

2 Hang a small mirror on the upper right-hand corner of your computer monitor. This will allow you to see who is standing behind you at any given time. Whenever someone approaches, just close your Internet window and switch back to that boring Excel file.

③ Change the font setting on the display of your computer screen to extra small. Mr. Boss won't be able to tell if you're working on that mail merge document or surfing Amazon.com for bargain lampshades.

④ Have all your friends create fake e-mail addresses for themselves with big corporate names in the screen name. This way, if Mr. Boss peeks over your shoulder to check what you're e-mailing, he'll see you are busy responding to client inquiries at, say, jennysmith@theWhiteHouse.com.

⑤ Turn your computer monitor so that it faces directly toward incoming sunlight from a nearby window. The ensuing glare will render anything on your screen invisible to passersby.

• DAMAGE CONTROL •

GETTING YOURSELF OUT OF THAT TANGLED WORLD WIDE WEB

If you have the misfortune of actually getting caught playing on the Internet at work, here are some job-saving strategies you can employ.

① *Caught Shopping Red-Handed:* Busy on eBay bidding on Genghis Khan's teeth when Mr. Boss suddenly appears over your shoulder? No problem. Just switch off your computer monitor so the screen goes blank and growl, "Darn! My computer keeps freezing. Guess I'll have to shut the whole thing down." Then, with the toe of your shoe, shut off the computer tower, and launch into a dramatic performance of shaking your head as though terribly confused, pulling at your hair, kicking the desk, and pretending to dial Tech Support.

② *The Porn Is as High as an Elephant's Eye:* Sneaking into a pornography website to pick up some new moves when Mr. Boss catches you in the act? No problem! Just turn to him with a look of utter exasperation on your face, then back at your screen, shake your head and scream indignantly, "If I get ONE MORE of these obscene spam mailings, I am going to have to ask you to report it to the authorities, sir. I am thoroughly disgusted and highly offended." He will be so worried he accidentally forwarded you that website when he was perusing it at lunch that he'll leave you alone. And you can go right back to investigating just how, exactly, that woman in the photo got her leg to go in that direction.

③ *Gotta Run:* Fess up and offer to make up the lost time . . . then conveniently come down with explosive diarrhea and need to go home.

HOW TO MAKE PERSONAL PHONE CALLS ON COMPANY TIME

A Smart Girl does not allow her job to interfere with her personal life. Here are a few easy ways to keep up with social calls on company time.

① Whenever Mr. Boss walks by your desk, put your friend on hold.

② Cup the telephone receiver with your hands as though you are holding an ice cream cone. (Yes, this would mean your ice cream cone has a long curly cord thing attached to it, but just use your imagination.) Whenever you speak, speak into your hands. Anything you say will be too garbled and muffled to be overheard by passers-by. (Of course, the listener on the other end might have trouble understanding you as well . . .)

③ Cry into the phone whenever Mr. Boss approaches. He will just figure you have received terrible news and would rather leave you alone than have to comfort such a whimpering simp.

④ Make all your personal calls from your cell phone in one hand while simultaneously carrying on business with your office phone in the other. The drawbacks are obvious, though. Unless you are extremely ambidextrous and highly skilled at double talk, you will inevitably end up confusing your calls and, thereby, telling the client you got "totally wasted last night" and your friend to invest in stock that doesn't exist.

⑤ Go to the desk of a coworker who is on vacation and make personal calls from his/her extension. This is a particularly useful tool when you need to make long distance calls to China.

A PENIS BY ANY OTHER NAME IS STILL A PENIS

So, what do you do if Mr. Boss catches you gabbing on the phone with your best friend Angie in Texas? Well, it's pretty hard to make, "Oh, my God, his penis was HOW big?" sound relevant to your job. But it *can* be done. More important, it *must* be done.

Introducing . . . the Word Switch. The art of swapping out "safe" words to cover for the inappropriate ones you are overheard saying on the job. None of what you claim you are saying will make any sense at all. But the crazier Mr. Boss thinks you are, the more likely he is to leave you alone to your phone call. All you need is a good grasp of the English language and some quiet time to think. (If you're a blonde, dye your hair brown so you can think harder.)

For example—back to your friend Angie. Here she is telling you all about her latest fling with the circus midget when Mr. Boss strolls by . . .

What Mr. Boss Thinks He Heard You Say: "Oh, my God! His penis was HOW big?"
What You Tell Mr. Boss He Actually Heard: "Um, my gut! It's peanuts by Hauptig?"

This works perfectly if you are a peanut company employee trying to branch out to German customers.

Moving on. Let's say you're chatting with Lucy in Latvia about your wild night out last night.

What Mr. Boss Thinks He Heard You Say: "I drank too much gin last night."
What You Tell Mr. Boss He Actually Heard: "I trained two munchkins last night."

Naturally, Mr. Boss will assume you were doing some volunteer work after hours on behalf of the company.

Let's say Mr. Boss overhears you having a fight with your boyfriend. Easy 'nuff!

What Mr. Boss Thinks He Heard You Say: "I'm gonna slit your throat while you sleep."
What You Tell Your Boss He Actually Heard: "I'm gonna snip your coat while you sweep."

Mr. Boss will think the world of you for offering to mend your boyfriend's clothing after a long day at work!

Caught bragging to a friend about all the office supplies you've been "borrowing" for your home? No problem!

What Mr. Boss Thinks He Heard You Say: "My boss is too dumb to notice the fax machine is missing."
What You Tell Mr. Boss He Actually Heard: "My pussy has two thumbs, two noses, and my washing machine is hissing."

Mr. Boss wouldn't dare interrupt you knowing you're dealing with a handicapped cat and home appliance carnage!

Think Mr. Boss might have heard you talking about him? Problem solved.

What Mr. Boss Thinks He Heard You Say: "My boss is an imbecile!"
What You Tell Mr. Boss He Actually Heard: "My God, it's a bicycle!"

And how can Mr. Boss help but be impressed with an employee trying to save on gas?

Or perhaps, Mr. Boss caught you on the phone with your gynecologist. Well, some antibiotics and a clever turn-of-phrase can unstick that sticky situation.

What Mr. Boss Thinks He Heard You Say: "I think he gave me chlamydia."

What You Tell Mr. Boss He Actually Heard: "I think he gave me the play *Medea.*"

Undoubtedy, Mr. Boss will appreciate your more cultured side.

Uh-oh. Angie is calling back to talk about your favorite movie star.

What Mr. Boss Thinks He Heard You Say: "Johnny Depp is sooooo hot."

What You Tell Mr. Boss He Actually Heard: "Chinese dip is sooooo hot."

This will inevitably get Mr. Boss hungry for lunch—and on the phone to Wang's Chinese Temple.

And what if you're busy telling Angie the office air conditioning is too high and your shirt is too sheer? Fear not!

What Mr. Boss Thinks He Heard You Say: "My nipples show through this shirt."

What You Tell Mr. Boss He Actually Heard: "Mike threw up on his shirt."

Ewwwwww. No one, not even Mr. Boss, wants to see puke in the office! He'll flee the scene before you can even begin talking about how your thong is riding up your butt!

• BRINGING OUT YOUR INNER SMART GIRL •

Now, you've gotten even with all the annoying, rude, and obnoxious people in your office. Even learned how to scam the company a bit.

"BLAH, BLAH": TOP FIVE MOST RIDICULOUS CORPORATE SPEAK PHRASES AND WHAT THEY REALLY MEAN

CORPORATE SPEAK
"I want to open up the channels for a productive dialogue."

TRANSLATION
"You're wrong, I'm right . . . so shut up."

CORPORATE SPEAK
"I want to see a proactive approach to our global agenda."

TRANSLATION
"I have no idea what I am doing here, so I'm just gonna use lots of big words and hope I fool everyone."

CORPORATE SPEAK
"We need to work on our strategic partnering to enhance our customer-facing value stream."

Now it's time to empower your Smart Girl spirit, so that even the worst day at work doesn't get the best of you.

Drag out the yoga mat you got free with the purchase of two loaves of bread, take a few deep breaths, and meditate on these, your new Smart Girl rules.

THE SMART GIRL WORKING COMMANDMENTS

1 *What Happens at Work, Stays at Work:* The key to happiness is never letting your job affect your personal life. Whether you have a roommate, a boyfriend, or a three-legged cat, make sure your problems at work remain just that: at work. Punch out at that time clock, shake off whatever bad memories you have of the day, and forget about them until tomorrow. Your home should be a safe haven where you experience nothing but joy, love, and reality television. General rule of thumb: any place you can be naked is a place you should not discuss work. Unless, of course, you're a stripper . . .

TRANSLATION
"Our sales record sucks, so if we don't fix this, we'll all be unemployed and eating cat food on the streets."

CORPORATE SPEAK
"Think outside the box."

TRANSLATION
"Have you ever had an original thought in your head, you idiot!"

CORPORATE SPEAK
"Put everything in writing."

TRANSLATION
"Put everything in writing, except anything having to do with stuff I don't want anyone to know about."

2 *Schedule an Office Bitch Fest:* Once a week invite your favorite coworkers to join you for drinks after work. No spouses, no outside friends, no relatives or pets allowed. This time together each week will give you and your colleagues a chance to bond, commiserate, and complain about work in a safe environment . . . over nachos and $1 draft beers nonetheless. Even the most miserable work week will be all the more bearable when you can look forward to the next evening out with equally miserable coworkers. Misery loves company . . . and bottomless margaritas.

③ *Surround Yourself with Love:* Hang photos of your favorite relatives, friends, and George Clooney around your desk to give you reason to *not* kill yourself each day.

④ *Institute Fun Office Traditions:* Inject a little fun into your office environment. Start a tradition of celebrating each colleague's birthday with cake and ice cream. Institute a rule that whoever goes on vacation must bring back desk souvenirs for the rest of the staff. Organize Secret Santa / Mysterious Messiah grab bags during the holiday season. Most people want to be happier in their workplace, but just don't know how to get the ball rolling like a Smart Girl does. You'd be surprised how contagious happiness can be!

⑤ *Decompress and De-Stress:* When work pressures have you feeling down, indulge a bit to ease the stress. Walk home. It'll give you some much-needed fresh air, a jolt of aerobic exercise, and a chance to window-shop. (Of course, if you live in Alaska, taking a long walk might get you eaten by a polar bear, but hey, you're the idiot who chose to live in the Final Frontier.) Or treat yourself to a gift: a new handbag or perhaps some tight designer jeans you'll have to starve yourself to fit into. Go to a movie and get your mind off your job and onto Brad Pitt's pectoral muscles. Visit the gym. Give yourself a facial. Paint your toenails blue. A Smart Girl knows that the key

> **"FAUX FRIENDLY": TOP FIVE "COMPLIMENTS" (FOR YOUR OFFICE NEMESIS)**
>
> ① "Wow, that's a very interesting hairdo you have. It really suits you."
> ② "Sorry to hear your boyfriend dumped you. But you'll find someone who really deserves you."
> ③ "That's one heck of an idea you've come up with for the project, and I'm gonna make sure the Boss knows it came entirely from you."
> ④ "Wow! You are just as attractive as you are intelligent."
> ⑤ "You're worth every penny we pay you."

to career happiness is rewarding herself for a job well done . . .
or at least a job done on time . . .

6   *Home Sweet Home:* Hang out with a homeless person.
Watching someone dig their next meal out of the garbage and
sleep in a cardboard box on the street will remind you that
things can always be worse.

PART THREE

Gal Pals

A Friend in Need Is a Good Reason to Screen Your Calls

• • •

Ten Signs You Are a Pushover with Your Friends

1. Girls Night Out means *Girls Night Out Until a Cute Guy Offers to Take Your Friend Home.*

2. Your home is Crash Central for depressed friends with nowhere else to go.

3. You are broke because you've loaned too much money to friends.

4. Your friends are so boring you need to get drunk just to get through dinner with them.

5. You can't remember the last time a friend asked how YOU were doing.

6. Your friends give you an ego-bust, rather than an ego boost.

7. You feel more like a babysitter than a friend.

8. You agree to wear a peach polyester hula skirt bridesmaid dress.

9. Your friend has more of your clothes in her closet than you do.

10. You're thinking about becoming a hermit.

They are simultaneously your best friends and your worst enemies. They bring both fits of laughter and waterfalls of tears into your life. They are the reason you get up in the morning, and the reason you hide under the covers and call in sick to work. In short, they are . . . (insert dramatic music here) . . . your girlfriends.

For better or worse these are the women who walk you through the most pivotal ups and downs of life. From family crises and dating disasters to career calamities and loves lost, you rely on these women to cheer you up when you are down, and tell you the truth so long as it doesn't hurt. In a perfect world, they would be . . . well, perfect. But even the best of gal pals has her flaws.

A girlfriend can make you laugh and make you cry. She can boost your ego, or crush it in a single blow. She simultaneously brightens your day and frustrates you to no end. She is the girl who never keeps a promise. The blob who bores you to tears. The man-hungry temptress who ditches you for a guy, and the thief who never returned the *Xanadu* DVD she borrowed. But still, you must deal with these gal pal idiosyncrasies because even mediocre friends are hard to find. (Why you even own a copy of *Xanadu* is the subject of another book entirely.)

Getting even with the gal pal who has done you wrong won't end your friendship . . . it'll actually save it!

CHAPTER 19

The Bad Judgment Girl

(Latin: *Painus in the arse-us*)

• OBSERVED BEHAVIOR IN NATURAL HABITAT •

This misguided soul is a victim of her own bad judgment. She has made a mess of her life and expects you to clean up after her on a regular basis. She will ask for your advice in a matter, then go and do the exact opposite of what you told her to do. She is the kind of girl who dates the hoodlum with the criminal record rather than the model citizen with the medical degree. The girl who has eighty pregnancy scares because she "forgot" to use birth control eighty times. The one who drives 130 mph in a Blind Children Crossing zone, and then calls you to bail her out of the speeding ticket she can't believe she got. In short, she is a walking disaster. Someone to whom you can never say, "Well, things certainly can't get worse!" because they can . . . and most certainly will.

• OFTEN HEARD SAYING •

"I can't believe I was so stupid!"

"Why does this always happen to me?"

"I need your advice."

"Hey, I'm in jail. Can you come down and get me?"

"This time I'm gonna do the smart thing!"

● WHY YOU MUST TAKE ACTION ●

Don't take offense here, but if your life were such a spectacular example of perfection, you wouldn't be reading this book, right? So, what makes you think you can afford to spend one more minute babysitting the Bad Judgment Girl? Yes, you dread whenever the phone rings because it might be her calling with yet another problem. But you have enough problems of your own. It's high time you focus on improving your own life and let this girl clean up after her own mess.

● IT'S REVENGE TIME! ●

The Bad Judgment Girl has been a unremitting headache long enough. Time to turn the tables and let her suffer the migraine for a change.

THE SUBTLE APPROACH

1. *I Need to See Some ID:* Get caller ID and screen all the Bad Judgment Girl's calls. . . . Why haven't you been doing that all along? Duh!

2. *Opposites Detract:* Since the Bad Judgment Girl is in the habit of asking for your advice and then doing the exact opposite of what you recommend, start giving HER bad advice. If she wants to know whether to accept the marriage proposal from that serial killer on Death Row or date the handsome, successful doctor she met at yoga, tell her to go for the Death Row killer. She'll be Mrs. Dr. Not-So-Bad Judgment Girl soon enough.

3. *You Did What?!* On the rare occasions when the Bad Judgment Girl does something right, scream out, "Oh man! I can't believe you screwed this up so badly!" It serves no purpose, but it'll be really funny to see the expression on her face.

THE NOT-SO-SUBTLE APPROACH

1. *¿Habla Espanol?* Every time the Bad Judgment Girl calls with her latest crisis, answer your phone in a thick Spanish accent. *"¿Que? ¿Que? No hablo Ingles."* No matter how many times she identifies herself, act as though you have no idea who she is. Then curse a lot and yell into the phone. After being cursed out in Spanish several times, she will eventually be too scared to call again. *¡Adios, amiga!*

2. *A, B, CC:* Every time the Bad Judgment Girl has a crisis, write down all the details and then e-mail them to everyone in your e-mail address book, including a CC: to her. She will be so devastated that you have revealed her latest screwup to everyone, she may just shut up. (Probably not, but it's worth a try.)

3. *A Sign of the Times:* Stick a sign on her back that reads, "I'm Stupid—and It's Contagious."

THE YOU'RE GOING TO HELL APPROACH

1. *His & Hermits:* Confine the Bad Judgment Girl to her own home. Lock the doors from the outside; cancel her phone service. There is just so much damage she can do to her life, and yours, from within those four walls.

2. *Doughn't Know Much About History:* Have the phone company transfer all incoming calls from the Bad Judgment Girl to Tony's Pizza Parlor on Main Street. Let Louie the dough boy help her with her latest problem!

3. *Career Daze:* Bring the Bad Judgment Girl to your nephew's Career Day at school and use her as an example of what children should *not* do with their lives.

• TOP THREE GIFTS TO GIVE THE BAD JUDGMENT GIRL •

1 A self-help book with all the pages glued together.

2 A bottle of pills.

3 A year's worth of visits to the shrink.

CHAPTER 20

The Mooch

(Latin: *Takerus of what is notus hersus*)

● OBSERVED BEHAVIOR IN NATURAL HABITAT ●

This creature is always "short on cash" or "out of toothpaste" or needs "a place to crash." Her bedroom is blooming with your music CDs, your makeup, and your books (which now look as though they have been trampled on by a herd of skittish elephants). Whenever she visits she eats her way through your refrigerator and runs up your phone bill with complete disregard for your financial situation. In short, she's a leech, sucking you dry.

● OFTEN HEARD SAYING ●

"Oh! I love your blouse. Can I borrow it?"

"Shoot. I forgot my wallet."

"I lost my keys. Mind if I crash here for the night?"

"Can I borrow your boyfriend?"

"Gee, I'm pretty sure I returned that to you already . . ."

● WHY YOU MUST TAKE ACTION ●

What is the point of bringing Chinese food home for dinner if the Mooch is going to suck your General Tso's chicken down her pipes before you've even grabbed the chopsticks? Why pay the full rent all by your lonesome when the Mooch is constantly sleeping on your couch? You didn't buy that iPod just to have her stick the headphones in her wax-ridden ears, or that leather skirt only to watch her squeeze her fatty hips into it, right? It's high time you take back what is rightfully yours (even if that leather skirt is a bit tight on you, too).

• IT'S REVENGE TIME! •

The key to getting even with the Mooch is making it impossible for her to get a hold of your belongings. Or if she does, make her pay for her debt in ways she never imagined.

THE SUBTLE APPROACH

1. *Sick in the Head:* Whenever the Mooch asks to borrow something, explain that you have already promised it to another friend . . . who is very, very sick in the hospital with a terminal illness. This will buy you a few months of respite at the very least. And she won't dare be pushy because, well, your imaginary friend is dying and all.

2. *To Borrow Is Another Day:* Begin asking to borrow the Mooch's things, but start small. Like, with her Celine Dion CDs. Then move up to her cutlery, her bathmat set, her television, maybe even her credit card if she's stupid enough to relinquish it. Then . . . and this is *muy importante* (that's Spanish for "very important" . . . or is it Polish for "my cheesecake"?) do not return any of it. Ever. This will level the playing field a bit.

3. *The Dewey Decimal System:* Just as the library does, begin charging overdue fines for "borrowed" items the Mooch walks off with. Your mittens, your DVDs, that bag of frozen bagels you've had in the fridge since 1996. And just as the library does, send her a cursory reminder e-mail stating something to the ef-

fect of, "You will be charged ten cents per day for every day borrowed item has not been returned." It's doubtful she'll ever pay the fines, but she sure will get annoyed with the e-mails.

THE NOT-SO-SUBTLE APPROACH

1. *Downsizing:* If the Mooch is always borrowing clothing from your wardrobe, an easy solution is to buy smaller clothes! She can't borrow what she can't fit into, right? Start shopping in the children's section of clothing stores. She won't be able to squeeze that sausagelike body into that infant-size linen suit for anything (of course, you won't either, but at least you'll break her of that nasty borrowing habit).

2. *The Decoy:* Whenever the Mooch asks to "borrow" something of yours, happily lend it to her. But make a few changes to the item first. Shoot some staples into your sweater. Switch the Metallica's *Greatest Hits* CD with your mother's *Tibetan Throat Singers: Greatest Hits.* Slip some rye bread into the whole wheat bag. Mismatch your books with dust jackets from other books. Swap your credit card for your library card and just handwrite the word, VISA across it. You get the idea.

3. *In the Big House:* Install a Lo Jack tracking device on anything the Mooch takes so that when she fails to return items in a duly fashion you can report the theft to the security company. They will send out an APB to the cops and she'll be arrested in no time.

THE YOU'RE GOING TO HELL APPROACH

1. *The Name of the Game:* She may have gotten your Chanel bag and stereo, but you, Smart Girl, are going to walk away with something the Mooch cannot do without, nor replace. Her identity. Under her name, open random bank accounts in for-

eign countries, apply for mortgages for houses she cannot afford, open a few credit cards and charge really embarrassing things like sex dolls to her account. Heck, why not establish a criminal record for her while you're at it?

❷ *The Nude You:* Join a nudist colony. She can't borrow what you don't wear.

❸ *Address the Issue:* Move. She can't mooch off you if she can't find you, right?

• TOP THREE GIFTS TO GIVE THE MOOCH •

❶ A pet snapping turtle.

❷ An expired gift card.

❸ An all expense paid vacation to a war zone.

CHAPTER 21

The Copy Cat

(Latin: *Friendus xeroxus*)

● OBSERVED BEHAVIOR IN NATURAL HABITAT. ●

This creature is basically your shadow, copying your clothing, your perfume, your job, and everything you do and say. She has not had an original thought in her entire life, and does whatever you do, whenever you do it, for however long you do it. If you quit your job, she quits her job. If you buy a hairless cat, she buys a hairless cat. If you have sex with six Venezuelan trapeze artists during a drunken one-night sta— Well, you get the idea.

● OFTEN HEARD SAYING ●

"Hey, I like your jacket."

"Where did you get that bag?"

"They just happened to have the exact same one you got on sale!"

"Wow! I love your apartment. What's the landlord's number?"

"Gee, I'd love to meet your parents. And then move into your childhood room."

• WHY YOU MUST TAKE ACTION •

You are an original. At least, you were *supposed* to be! But how in the world can you distinguish yourself in this life if your friend is your living, breathing clone? (Though not nearly as cute, of course.) What is the point of developing your own unique style (if that's what you call that beaded skirt you bought and that hairdo you've been sporting that looked really good on Sharon Stone—Sharon Stone being the operative words here) if the Copy Cat is going to replicate your look and get all the attention? Why have a boyfriend if you know she's going to date him as well? You are your own woman and should be treated as such. (Why she picked you as a role model is a mystery, anyway—doesn't she know you bought this book?)

• IT'S REVENGE TIME! •

Since the Copy Cat has made a career of duplicating your every move, let her replication tendencies dig this creature right into her own worst nightmare.

THE SUBTLE APPROACH

1. *Sack It to Her:* Begin wearing clothing made entirely of burlap. The Copy Cat will do the same, and look really stupid doing it. Of course, you won't look so hot, either. But this isn't about you, now is it?

2. *A Community Un-Affair:* Sign up to volunteer for the day cleaning up a park in a really dangerous neighborhood. She'll do the same. Then don't show up.

3. *Scent of a Woman:* Wear a perfume made with ingredients the Copy Cat is horribly allergic to. Ingredients that will make her skin break out into a vicious rash or cause her to sneeze uncontrollably.

THE NOT-SO-SUBTLE APPROACH

1. *The Bee in Her Bonnet:* Become Amish. The Copy Cat won't last three weeks without television or an automatic can opener.

2. *Copyous Interruptus:* Start copying the Copy Cat. This will result in a stalemate of sorts as she copies you, who are already copying her, who has already copied you. Eventually, the Copy Cat will get bored and move on to one of her other, "more original" friends. Or she'll just go crazy and end up in an institution . . . where again, everyone is wearing the same thing so she's just as screwed.

3. *Your Copyrights:* Copyright all your clothes. Put that little copyright ©2007 symbol on everything you have. If she shows up wearing the same outfit or hairdo, shake your head and state that you're going to have your lawyer begin the lawsuit straight away.

THE YOU'RE GOING TO HELL APPROACH

1. *Up Jaws!* Go swimming in shark-infested waters. The Copy Cat will follow suit and thereby get eaten. Or at the very least, lose a limb or two. Of course, the downside is that you may not get out alive either. But then again, maybe you will? (Probably not, but maybe.)

2. *G-String Her Along:* Become a stripper.

3. *Pot Luck:* Give the appearance of having developed a dependency on an illicit narcotic substance. Suddenly lose a lot of weight, dust your skin with yellow powder to make yourself look jaundiced, and let the Copy Cat "catch" you snorting a white substance in the bathroom. She will soon take up a real drug

habit of her own and begin looking like real crap in no time, as well. As you drop her off at rehab confess to her that you were simply snorting confectioners sugar. It's too late for her and her arm tracks to turn back from the rehab clinic now. That gives you thirty days of freedom from her copy cat ways.

• TOP THREE GIFTS TO GIVE THE COPY CAT •

1. A photocopier.

2. A bottle of old-fashioned Coke with a note attached that reads, "The Original."

3. A string of paper dolls with a note that says, "Way to stand out in the crowd!"

CHAPTER 22

The Boring (but Obligatory) Family Friend

(Latin: *Friendus by defaultus*)

• OBSERVED BEHAVIOR IN NATURAL HABITAT •

This creature is usually the daughter of your mother's best friend or your father's boss, and thereby a staple at all family events. Which totally sucks for you because you can't stand her. Whether she's a librarian, a tollbooth clerk, or in the dried flower arrangement business, she is so boring you need to take an upper just to get through an evening with her. She is the reason you spent your vacation in Puerto Rico at the International Museum of Yarn rather than hang gliding, and it is because of this blob of tedium that you ended up playing Monopoly all day by the pool rather than scuba diving in Mexico. A night out with her means suffering through sappy Disney films rather than the latest slasher flicks. She is the pooper of every party—sipping a glass of milk while everyone else is doing tequila shots in their underwear. And yet, it is impossible to extricate yourself from her presence because of your darned parents!

• OFTEN HEARD SAYING •

"It's a long story . . . I'll start from the beginning."

"Hey, hey! Are you listening to me? Wake up!"

"Do you want to go to the park with me to feed the pigeons?"

"Nah, I don't want to do that."

"Nah, I don't want to do that, either."

• WHY YOU MUST TAKE ACTION •

A friend is supposed to enhance your life, not make you want to end it. But the Boring (but Obligatory) Family Friend is proving to be a veritable noose around your neck, killing you slowly with her mind-numbing conversation and inactive lifestyle. The more time you spend with her, the more boring you are becoming. If you don't take action quickly, you will soon be one of those people who considers bird-watching a spectator sport.

• IT'S REVENGE TIME! •

Because of the family ties that bind, this faux gal pal is inescapable. Or is she? If you could only find a way . . . or say, nine ways . . . to turn your family against her . . . why, then you'd almost never have to see her, right? Except for your birthday of course. But that's all right—you like getting gifts. Even from boring people.

THE SUBTLE APPROACH

1. *Let's Give Thanks:* When Thanksgiving and her inevitable visit arrives, tell the Boring (but Obligatory) Family Friend that your family is observing an all-nude holiday this year. Instruct her to arrive buck naked to dinner "just as the rest of us are doing." Then sit back and laugh as Grandma Mimi forbids the Boring (but Obligatory) Family Friend and her hairy nipples to return next year.

2. *It's a Date:* Give the Boring (but Obligatory) Family Friend a calendar that is one day off. This way, she will be one day off for all the major family holiday celebrations. And that means one

heck of a great year for you! (But swap it out for a correct calendar when your birthday is approaching, of course.)

❸ *In a Land Fart, Fart Away:* Whenever the Boring (but Obligatory) Family Friend is visiting, let loose the stinkiest fart you can force out of your sphincter. Soon enough she'll start conveniently having to "miss" visits.

THE NOT-SO-SUBTLE APPROACH

❶ *Adopt a New Practice:* Think about it. The single thing that is tying you to the Boring (but Obligatory) Family Friend is your family. They are the reason you are forced to keep company with this annoying gnat. So, get rid of the family, and you get rid of the annoying gnat. Contact a lawyer and file for emancipation from your parents. This will absolve you of all family-oriented obligations—from the tedious birthday parties and tree-trimming affairs, to the graduation celebrations and Flag Day barbecues.

❷ *Are Jew Catholic?* Whatever the Boring (but Obligatory) Family Friend's religion, begin observing a different religious holiday. Just when Christmas arrives and you are about to be dragged off to her house for the annual tree-decorating ceremony, convert to Judaism. She'll be too afraid of burning in Catholic Hell to stay in the room as you light your portable menorah and chant from the Torah. Likewise, if she is Jewish, arrive for the annual family Seder with a giant cake in the shape of Baby Jesus.

❸ *Zippity Do Dah, Zippity Zap:* Install an electric fence around your family's property. Every time the Boring (but Obligatory) Family Friend rings the front doorbell, she will be zapped with a high dose of electricity.

THE YOU'RE GOING TO HELL APPROACH

1 *The Montagues vs. the Capulets:* Start a fight between your respective mothers. For instance, make a comment to the Boring (but Obligatory) Family Friend that your mother thinks her mother has had "some work done" on her face. This will inevitably get back to her mother, and all Hell will break loose. The worse the false rumor you spread, the longer the duration of the cat fight that will ensue. And that means no annoying visits with the Boring (but Obligatory) Family Friend.

2 *The Boobonic Plague:* Contract a highly contagious disease like leprosy or the Black Death (available for purchase online at various sites). The Boring (but Obligatory) Family Friend won't want to come over any time soon for fear of developing full-body blisters or losing a finger.

3 *Liver Free or Die:* Inform the Boring (but Obligatory) Family Friend that you are suffering from a serious medical condition and require an organ transplant. Then ask her to be the donor. This will probably be the last time you hear from the girl.

● TOP THREE GIFTS TO GIVE THE BORING (BUT OBLIGATORY) FAMILY FRIEND ●

1 A Monopoly board with all the pieces missing.

2 A Christmas fruit cake.

3 A one-way ticket to the North Pole.

CHAPTER 23

The Social Parasite

(Latin: *Friendus leechus*)

• OBSERVED BEHAVIOR IN NATURAL HABITAT •

You throw a little party at your house and invite a select group of friends. Before you know, not only has all the onion dip been devoured but the Social Parasite has crashed the gig and honed in on all your pals. Rather than going out and getting her own friends, she simply exchanges phone numbers and e-mail addresses with *your* friends. And soon she's road-tripping to Canada with your best friend . . . without you.

• OFTEN HEARD SAYING •

"Oh, I just assumed I was invited."

"Hey, I really like your friend. Can I have her number?"

"What about her e-mail address and fax number?"

"Oh, I meant to invite you. Must have just forgot. Sorry."

"Hey, when's your office Christmas party?"

• WHY YOU MUST TAKE ACTION •

It wouldn't make much sense for you to cash your paycheck and hand a large portion of it to someone else, would it? No, of course not. But that is precisely what you are doing, in theory, when you let the Social Parasite steal your friends. You have worked hard to nurture the friendships you have made, and must not let this thief of pals reap the fruits of your labor. You sure as heck didn't make friends with that rich chick who owns the villa in Venice so that the Social Parasite can suck down free manicotti all summer, now did you?

● IT'S TIME FOR REVENGE! ●

When dealing with the Social Parasite it is essential that you block every attempt she makes to socialize with your people. Get in her way like a road block on the highway. (But no need to wear that ugly yellow tape stuff . . . that'll just look stupid on you.)

THE SUBTLE APPROACH

1. *The Good, the Bad, and the Really Fugly:* Begin socializing only with people who have disgusting skin problems and facial ticks, problems controlling their bodily functions, and bad breath. This way the Social Parasite won't be so inclined to pick from your crop. Or borrow your lip gloss for that matter.

2. *Ghetto Life, Will Ya?* Uh-oh. She did it again, huh? Invited herself to another one of your social engagements. No problem. Simply give the Social Parasite the wrong address for the event . . . preferably one in a really, really bad neighborhood . . . very, very late at night.

3. *What's in a Name?* Whenever you bump into the Social Parasite on the street while with another friend, you are at risk of her stealing that friend away. So, make the introductions impossible by refusing to give up your other friend's name. Just say, "Um, oh yeah, and this is my friend." Then quickly run away.

THE NOT-SO-SUBTLE APPROACH

● *Hand Jive:* Make friends with a bunch of hearing-impaired people. Because the Social Parasite doesn't know sign language she will be unable to communicate with your friends, let alone steal them. The added plus? She won't know when you guys are talking about her.

● *Crazy for You:* Introduce the Social Parasite to your "new best friend" and suggest they begin hanging out together. What she doesn't know is that this new friend is a complete psycho with serious separation anxiety issues.

● *You've Got Hate Mail:* Whenever the Social Parasite asks for your friend's e-mail address, happily provide her with a fake one you have manufactured on your own Internet account. When she e-mails your friend to make plans for dinner one night without you, simply fire back with the following message, "PLEASE LEAVE ME ALONE. I DO NOT LIKE YOU AND DO NOT WISH TO BE CONTACTED BY YOU EVER AGAIN, YOU CRAZY LOON!" She won't e-mail much after that. Or be able to find her dignity.

THE YOU'RE GOING TO HELL APPROACH

● *Les-Bi-Friends:* Whenever you see the Social Parasite moving in on one of your girlfriends, pull your girlfriend aside and explain that the Social Parasite is an aggressive lesbian who doesn't take no for an answer.

● *Gang Green:* Start hanging out with a violent women's street gang. Really toughies. The kind of ghetto girls who bench-press small children and crush soda cans on their foreheads. The Social Parasite will inevitably want to join the gang (those jackets are just too cool!), and that's when she will find out that initiation involves getting beaten in an alley with a pitchfork by the rest of the girls.

③ *Lady MacBeast:* The next time the Social Parasite meets one of your friends for drinks without including you, murder your friend and frame the Social Parasite for the crime. It's easier than it sounds. Just plant her fingerprints all over the big butcher knife you will stab your friend with fifty or so times . . . you know, the knife with her initials engraved on the handle . . . then leave it at the crime scene with a photo of the culprit, her phone number, address, and a note attached that reads, "Dear Police. I did it."

● TOP THREE GIFTS TO GIVE THE SOCIAL PARASITE ●

① A computer game of Solitaire.

② A table setting for one.

③ A pet leech.

CHAPTER 24

The "It's All About Me" Friend

(Latin: *Egotisticus brattus*)

She talks AT you rather than TO you, employs the use of the word "I" about ten times as frequently as she does "you," and believes that the entire world revolves around her. She thinks nothing of calling you at all hours of the night when she is having a problem but is the first person to hang up on you when you're having a bad day. If the topic of conversation isn't about her, she isn't interested. As a matter of fact, you could be on fire in the middle of her living room, your face melting and your hair a giant ball of flames, and she'd be more worried about her new curtains burning than about *your* imminent charring.

• OFTEN HEARD SAYING •

"Well, *I* think . . ."

"You would not believe the day I've had!"

"Enough about you; let's talk about me."

"Huh? Did you say something?"

"I'm just way too giving a person, that's my problem."

● WHY YOU MUST TAKE ACTION ●

Somewhere in between sharing crayons in kindergarten and graduating high school, you went from being the "It's All About Me" Friend's pal to well, her bitch. Aren't you sick of every conversation revolving around this girl who sports an ego the size of Dolly Parton's boobs? Aren't you tired of acquiescing (yes, we use some mighty impressive SAT-type words in this book, don't we?) to her every want and need, often at the expense of your own? Surely your needs, your feelings account for something! Friendships are supposed to be a two-way street, so avoid any more hit and runs by putting this friend in her place.

● IT'S REVENGE TIME! ●

The key to getting even with the "It's All About Me" Friend is making her the center of attention . . . just not the *kind* of attention she wants. After being the victim of these revenge tactics, this girl with the golden ego will be more than happy to focus on you for a change.

THE SUBTLE APPROACH

❶ *The Cough-y Clutch:* Every time the "It's All About Me" Friend says the word "I," let out a hacky cough. Subconsciously, she will begin to associate the word "I" with drool and airborne germs. And that means she may, just may, not say "I" so much.

❷ *Fuhgeddaboutit!* Whenever the "It's All About Me" Friend forgets your birthday, conveniently "forget" hers.

❸ *Just the Facts Ma'am:* Any time you find yourself the unwilling audience to yet another one of the "It's All About Me" Friend's long-winded monologues about herself, interrupt her to clarify minute, irrelevant details. For instance, if she's rambling on about what a great date she just had with some guy, ask her something like, "At the restaurant, did the forks have three or four prongs?" Do this every 15 seconds or so until she just gives up the fantasy of finishing her speech.

THE NOT-SO-SUBTLE APPROACH

❶ *Just Kid-ing:* Whenever the "It's All About Me" Friend is about to dump you for some cute guy at a bar say, "Sure I can get home okay. But are your four kids gonna be all right all alone tonight? Especially, little Matty, the retarded one?" Even the horniest of men will move on to the other end of the bar.

❷ *A Birthday Suprise:* At her next birthday party, just when the "It's All About Me" Friend is about to blow out the candles on her cake and make a lengthy speech about herself and how great she is, run up to the top of the stairs and hurl yourself down. Break as many bones as possible before hitting the landing. This will quickly shift the attention away from the "It's All About Me" Friend and onto you—and that makes for one Unhappy Birthday!

❸ *The Bad News Is:* Mail the "It's All About Me" Friend a DVD collection of newsreels featuring footage of natural disasters. You know, people getting blown away in hurricanes, sucked into tornadoes, drowned in raging rapids, burned alive in forest fires. Attach a card that reads, "Now, what were you saying about having a bad day?"

THE YOU'RE GOING TO HELL APPROACH

❶ *Fleshing Out Your System:* For your next vacation together take the "It's All About Me" Friend to an all-inclusive resort on a remote island in the Pacific that happens to be inhabited by cannibals. When she forces you to sit through that touristy puppet show at the local coconut hut, she's the one who will end up beef stew. (Mostly because you put a sign on her back that reads, "Eat Me—Not Her." Your meals are already included.)

② *A Very Taxing Situation:* Report the "It's All About Me" Friend to the IRS. She has no problem bragging to you for hours on end about all the cash tips she makes each year at work, right? Well, surely that government tax auditor would be more than happy to hear more about those?

③ *Stocking Stuffers:* Give the "It's All About Me" Friend a really bad stock tip. Like to invest all her savings in that company that has invented a toilet bowl / snow cone making machine.

• TOP THREE GIFTS TO GIVE THE "IT'S ALL ABOUT ME" FRIEND •

① A milk carton with her photo under the "Missing" side of the box.

② A button that reads, "Friends Forever . . . as Long as We're Talking About Me."

③ A pet tarantula with really big fangs.

CHAPTER 25

The Preachy Social Activist

(Latin: *Rebel with too many causeus*)

● OBSERVED BEHAVIOR IN NATURAL HABITAT ●

One of the more bothersome creatures in the friendship category, this freak is always on some crusade or other. Be it saving the platypus or educating people on the dangers of hair spray to the ozone layer, or clothing the homeless and feeding the poor, this Birkenstock-wearing, tree-saving, vegetarian gnat of a human being honestly thinks she can save the world all by herself. Her refrigerator is packed with organic fruits, vegetables, soy milk, and tofu, and she gives you really cheap gifts like hair clips made out of recycled soda cans and lifetime memberships to the Sierra Club. Her home is filled with PETA posters and pictures of Bob Geldoff posing with a bunch of ugly kids from poor countries. And worst of all? She doesn't shave her armpits!

● OFTEN HEARD SAYING ●

"Turnips are people, too, dammit!"

"You really shouldn't use mouse traps. They're cruel."

"Oh, no thanks. I don't eat anything that has a face."

"Tell me that's not leather you're wearing!"

"Give peace a chance."

• WHY YOU MUST TAKE ACTION •

Having a friend who is busy saving the world not only makes you look bad, but totally sucks the joy out of your life. The Preachy Social Activist has ruined one too many birthdays for you by bringing a tofu and soy icing cake. She is constantly lecturing you about everything you do wrong. How you shouldn't use toilet paper because you are "killing innocent trees." Why you can't order a Big Mac from McDonald's because "cows are people, too." How your hair spray is single-handedly killing the ozone layer. In this great competition we call life, how can you possibly compete with someone who spends her vacations digging irrigation ditches with the Peace Corps and refuses to eat baby lettuce because the "mommy and daddy lettuces would miss it." You happen to *like* hurting the environment and eating innocent animals. And gosh darn it, you have the right to!

• IT'S REVENGE TIME! •

Saving the planet, curing poverty, feeding the homeless. All well and good. But not when they interfere with your social life.

THE SUBTLE APPROACH

1. *The Energy Crisis:* When the Preachy Social Activist asks you to house-sit while she is in the Galapagos Islands saving an amoeba from extinction, leave all the lights on in her home twenty-four hours a day. Her fellow preachy social activist friends won't be so pleased with her when they discover she is to blame for the local blackout.

2. *Baby Face:* Paste pictures of little animal faces on all the Preachy Social Activist's frozen vegetable dinners.

3. *The Last Frontier:* Buy the Preachy Social Activist stock in the Alaskan Pipeline.

THE NOT-SO-SUBTLE APPROACH

❶ *Habitat for Inhumanity:* Inform the Preachy Social Activist that, having been so inspired by her social awareness, you have decided to begin building houses for the less fortunate. Invite her to join you. Hook her up with a small plot of land, hammers, nails, a few buzz saws, ladders, and a sandblaster or two. Once the house is built, move into it. (Just make sure she did the plumbing first.)

❷ *Home Is Where the Heartless Is:* If the Preachy Social Activist is so interested in helping the homeless, why not help her make them feel right at home? Invite all the homeless people in the neighborhood to spend the night at *her* house. See how generous she feels after two dozen winos raid her refrigerator, stink up her sheets, try on her clothing, and run up her cable bill with premium movie channel charges.

❸ *Passing the Bug:* If the Preachy Social Activist insists on treating all life as equal, right down to the little bugs on the street, then bring a carload of cockroaches to her house and set them free. She'll be forced to choose between spraying pesticide and doing the La Cucaracha dance.

THE YOU'RE GOING TO HELL APPROACH

❶ *The Bump-Her Sticker:* Place a "Proud Owner of a Baby Seal Jogging Suit" bumper sticker on the Preachy Social Activist's car when she isn't looking. She'll be well on her way half across country to the annual Save the Seals convention before she figures out why everyone is trying to run her off the road.

❷ *Pleased to Meat Ya!* Secretly replace the Preachy Social Activist's tofu burger with a real hamburger.

❸ *Quilty as Charged:* Take that blanket the Preachy Social Activist knitted you and cut it up into pieces. Use the jagged patches as placemats when she comes over for dinner. When she freaks out at the sight of her gorgeous blanket in shreds, innocently remark that you were simply trying to recycle.

• TOP THREE GIFTS TO GIVE THE PREACHY SOCIAL ACTIVIST •

❶ A fur coat.

❷ A lifetime supply of A.1. Steak Sauce.

❸ The largest SUV on the market.

CHAPTER 26

The Flake

(Latin: *The no showus*)

• OBSERVED BEHAVIOR IN NATURAL HABITAT •

This creature is just wonderful at making fun plans with you. Only trouble is she NEVER KEEPS THEM! She is the first to come up with a great idea, and the last to actually go through with it. She cancels on Girls Night Out plans, shows up three days late to your basket-weaving class graduation, and pretty much leaves you hanging on a regular basis. She is the most fun friend you have, but totally unreliable. It's actually a wonder she even showed up in this book. We were sure she'd flake out on that, too.

• OFTEN HEARD SAYING •

"Oh, did we have plans?"

"Sorry, I woke up late."

"Yes, of course I'll be there!"

"Oooh! I have a great idea for something fun to do."

"Why are you in such a bad mood?"

• WHY YOU MUST TAKE ACTION •

Remember that trip to Egypt the Flake promised she would go on with you? How you waited four hours baking in the sun in front of the Sphinx only to find out she decided to stay home . . . in the United States? Oh, and remember the time she promised to water your plants and you returned to a house of dead ferns? Yes, the Flake flakes out on everything. As big as her mouth is, her word means absolutely nothing. If you can't rely on her to bring in the mail, what makes you think she'll be around to empty your bedpan when you get really old and needy?

• IT'S REVENGE TIME! •

The best way to get even with the Flake is to give her a taste of her own medicine. Mess with her plans, complicate her schedule, and inconvenience her until she begins to value your time a bit more.

THE SUBTLE APPROACH

1 *The Full Dance Card:* Any time the Flake tries to make plans with you, tell her you are already busy. Even if the highlight of your evening is going to be unloading the dishwasher, play hard-to-get. She'll be so excited when you finally are free for a night that she'll make sure to show up.

2 *Where the Cell Are You?* Whenever the Flake goes AWOL, dial her cell every two minutes and leave hysterical messages. "Where are you? Are you okay? I'm worried about you. You didn't show up!"

3 *The Wrong Time Heals All Wounds:* Set the Flake's watch ahead by an hour. This way she will actually be on time to meet you. At least until daylight saving time rolls around. Then you're back to square one.

THE NOT-SO-SUBTLE APPROACH

❶ *Missing You:* Every time the Flake fails to show up, call the police and report the Flake missing. While the search party is rummaging through the thickets of the woods in search of her body, plaster MISSING posters with her photograph all over the neighborhood and get yourself on the local news at least once, bawling uncontrollably, begging for her safe return.

❷ *Abushed:* Whenever the Flake is late to meet you at a designated place, hide behind some bushes until she arrives. Let her sit there feeling self-conscious for a good twenty minutes or so, as people point and laugh at the pathetic girl who got stood up. Then saunter on down the street and act as though you are right on time.

❸ *The Un-Peaceful Corps:* Sign both of you up for a month overseas with the Peace Corps. Just as the plane is about to leave the gate, grab your carry-on luggage (stuffed with newspaper of course) and jump off the plane. The Flake will be well over Somalia before she figures out you're not coming back. And that means she'll be peeing in a clay pot in some thatched roof hut for the next month all by her lonesome.

THE YOU'RE GOING TO HELL APPROACH

❶ *Labor Pains:* Wait until the Flake goes into labor with her first child and is depending on you to drive her to the hospital. Then keep getting the directions wrong, driving in endless circles as she screams in agony in the backseat. Do this until she is forced to give birth in a McDonald's parking lot.

❷ *Coma-Toast:* Kick the Flake in the kidneys until one of them fails. Then, as a gesture of goodwill, offer to give her one of yours to make up for the "incident." On the day of the operation, instead of going to the hospital for the surgery, go spend the day at the movie theater. She'll get awfully cold sitting in that operating room all day in a paper gown.

❸ *Don't Be a Quitter:* Encourage the Flake to resign her job because you can get her a position at your firm that pays double what she makes, with eight weeks' vacation and a company expense account to boot. Wait until she quits her job, cashes out her pension, and cancels her medical insurance before you tell her you were just kidding.

• TOP THREE GIFTS TO GIVE THE FLAKE •

❶ An alarm clock.

❷ A daily organizer that bites her if she misses an appointment.

❸ A box of Corn Flakes cereal.

CHAPTER 27

Smart Girl Tricks of the Trade

How to Get Even by Getting Over

● HOW TO PICK A GAY BACK-UP BUD ●

Ah, the Gay Back-Up Bud. Just like a good pair of Italian leather boots, every Smart Girl must have one. And if your Gay Back-Up Bud is Italian, then more power to you!

He is the perfect accessory for the Smart Girl who needs it all: cute, physically fit, and, unlike your boyfriend, willing to walk your pink poodle in public. He is thrilled to be your date at weddings when your boyfriend is out of town, not to mention accompany you to those dreaded college reunions, when your boyfriend would simply be too embarrassing to bring along. A perfectly groomed shoulder to cry on, a skilled chef when you crave a decent béarnaise sauce, this godsend will happily sit through a Meg Ryan movie marathon (twice), help you organize your closets, and even touch up your roots! And the best part is, the Gay Back-Up Bud is not, by any stretch of the imagination, after sex. At least, not with you. (Maybe with your brother . . . but we digress.)

Yes, ever since *Will & Grace* skyrocketed its homo-friendly humor to the top of the Nielsen ratings, Smart Girls have been shopping high and low for the ideal Gay Back-Up Bud. But not just any gay man can serve as your Gay Back-Up Bud. A worthy candidate must meet some important criteria. Find a gay guy who matches this mold, and you will have the best guy gal pal ever. Not to mention someone to make you one heck of a delicious soufflé.

THE GAY BACK-UP BUD MUST BE

1. *Unemployed or Work Flexible Hours:* A gay guy who has career obligations does not a good Gay Back-Up Bud make. A worthy candidate must be available to you all hours of the day, for whatever companion emergencies may arise. From joining you at the office holiday party, to driving you to the airport and steam-cleaning your rug, the Gay Back-Up Bud must be on call 24/7.

2. *Single:* A romantic relationship will inevitably get in the way of the Gay Back-Up Bud's ability to serve your needs. So, in reviewing potential candidates consider only those who have no ties to significant others. Best to look for a gay guy who, while not entirely ugly, is slightly on the homely side. The less appealing he is to his own sex, the more use he will be to you.

3. *Independently Wealthy:* The Gay Back-Up Bud is supposed to enhance your social life, not restrict it. And since your salary is never gonna buy you tickets to Paris, best to find an independently wealthy gay guy to take you. Or at the very least, a gay guy whose very rich parents are very terminally ill. Then you can vamp all over the world with his inheritance. And that makes any vacation a heck of a lot more fun!

4. *Somewhat Masculine:* Although you by no means need to find a gay guy who can dismantle and reassemble a Ford Mustang, it is in your best interest to employ a Gay Back-Up Bud who does not look, act, or sound particularly gay. Shoot for a homosexual who speaks without a lisp and doesn't wear mascara. Rule of thumb: if he looks like Boy George did in the '80s, stay away. Bottom line, you should always be the prettier one in the pair.

• DAMAGE CONTROL •

WHEN YOU FALL FOR YOUR GAY BACK-UP BUD

So, things have been going along just fine with the Gay Back-Up Bud. He keeps you laughing, enjoys all the same cultural activities you do, and has charmed the house coat off your mother. But suddenly, you find yourself strangely attracted to this boy with the French manicure and ironed jeans. You dream of his naked body against yours, and wonder what it would be like to kiss him.

Well, SNAP OUT OF IT!

The dude is gayer than Liberace at a Village People concert. He may hug you when you're sad and French-braid your hair perfectly. But your Gay Back-Up Bud does not, nor will he ever, want anything to do with your vagina! So, forget whatever little fantasy your pea brain has cooked up about his suddenly deciding he's straight, woman! He may be willing to help you shop for bras and practice yoga exercises. But he sure as heck isn't interested in licking your breasts or making a baby.

You need to banish whatever dream you have heterosexualizing your Gay Back-Up Bud *toute de suite*. (That's French for "right away" . . . or is it Aramaic for "lamppost"?)

Here are some really good reasons to *not* be attracted to your Gay Back-Up Bud:

① A guy who can make cream puffs is not a guy who can stop a mugger from stealing your purse . . . as a matter of fact, your Gay Back-Up Bud is probably the one carrying the purse!

② You can never trust a gay boyfriend alone in your closet.

③ Dating a gay guy means being banished to a life of low-carb diets and wine spritzers.

④ Are you really ready to commit to a man who wants your wedding song to be "Somewhere Over the Rainbow"?

⑤ Say good-bye to watching football games and NASCAR races. Say hello to season tickets to the international synchronized swimming competition.

⑥ Gay guys are utterly useless when it comes to dealing with mice infestations.

⑦ Gay guys can be really, really bitchy.

⑧ His whole life has been focused on the art of pleasing the penis. . . . A lot of good that will do *you* in bed.

⑨ By association alone, you will become a member of the Fruit of the Month Club.

⑩ Gay guys spend a lot of time with their mothers.

• HOW TO BE A BRIDESMAID •

Ah, bridesmaid duty. One of the most dreaded acts of service you will have to perform in a friendship. It means wearing a dress that resembles a nursing home tablecloth, suffering through costly bachelorette parties, tedious rehearsal dinners, fattening cake tastings and lengthy religious ceremonies. It means doting over your friend for a solid six months, a friend who is either marrying the wrong man for her or the right man for you. And all you have to show for your commitment to this white dress–wearing brat is a mammoth credit card bill and stupid parting gift she bought with the spare change she found in the sofa cushions while cleaning.

So how about giving a little back to the bratty bride who has made your life a living Hell, eh? She may be the one getting all the wedding gifts. But you're the one getting revenge!

THE BRIDAL GOWN FITTING

Being a bridesmaid means being forced to spend several of your weekends perusing bridal shops, sifting through racks of puffy white dresses that resemble polyester meringues, and oohing and ahhing over every gown the Bratty Bride tries on. So, pick out the most unflattering dress you can find on the "Irregular" rack and write the name "Vera Wang" on the label. If the Bratty Bride balks at the missing right sleeve or coffee stains dotting the waistline, explain it is the "newest look." If she questions the crooked hem or see-through top, tell her "It's all the rage." The Bratty Bride will walk down the aisle looking like the biggest fashion faux pas since Bjork wore that swan dress to the Grammy's.

THE BACHELORETTE PARTY

Put in charge of throwing the bachelorette party? Stick it to the Bratty Bride by organizing a fun-filled day of volunteering at a soup kitchen! Or throw the party at the local library, or host the shindig at your place and then conveniently trick all the girls into painting your living room in between party games. As long as you tape a few streamers on the wall and blow up some balloons, the Bratty Bride really can't complain, now can she?

THE BRIDESMAID DRESS

Don't like the dress the Bratty Bride is making you wear? Simple. On the day of the wedding, only five minutes prior to her romantic walk down the aisle, spill a pitcher of cranberry juice all over yourself. Just as she is about to collapse from anxiety, conveniently pull out that gorgeous Vera Wang you "happen to have" on you. The Bratty Bride would rather send you down the aisle in that than buck naked.

THE PHOTOS

Posing for wedding party photos. It means baking in the hot sun with your makeup melting off your face. It means being awkwardly positioned in painful poses next to the least attractive of the groom's ushers. So get some fun out of this otherwise miserable ordeal. Right before the wedding photographer clicks the shutter, step on the hem of the Bratty Bride's dress with your heel, just enough to make her dress tilt and expose her bra strap in all the photos. Do rabbit ears behind the Bratty Bride's mother. Slide the groom's hand over your breast. Stick your tongue in the father of the bride's ear. These photos will never make the wedding album. But oh, they will most certainly make the Internet!

THE STUPID PARTING GIFT

The Bratty Bride is morally obligated to give each member of her wedding party a gift. This piece of crap is supposed to compensate for the expenses you have laid out for her bachelorette party, the dress, the shoes, the wedding gift, the bridal shower. But it never does. At best, the Bratty Bride will give you a cheap charm necklace with the wrong initials in it. At worst, she'll give you a DVD of her wedding. So, take whatever stupid gift you get, fake Jesus Christ's autograph on it, and auction it off on the Internet.

THE THANK-YOU CARDS

Grab some Wite-Out and sneak into the Bratty Bride's thank-you card stationery box. Putting your best artistic foot forward carefully replace the word "Thank" with the letters, "F", "U", "C" . . . you see where this is going. With 200 plus cards to address, personalize, and mail, the already exhausted Bratty Bride will not be paying attention to the preprinted words. And that means 200 plus rather offensive thank-you/f—— you cards will be going out to all her guests. Even Father MacPherson. And four letters words do NOT go over well with men of the cloth.

• HOW TO GET BACK AT THE ANNOYING NEW MOTHER •

Your best friend just had a baby. You should be happy for her. But ever since that squirming, gurgling, squishy Thing weaseled its way into the world, your friendship has suffered. Gone are the late-night dinners and chick-flick marathons, the wild Vegas weekends and shopping excursions to the mall. Now Girls Night Out means watching that wiggling Thing pick its nose in the sand box, or listening to the Annoying New Mother praise the wonders of the Diaper Genie. You cannot remember the last time your girl talk wasn't cut short by "nap time" or "burp time," and you are sick and tired of watching your friend whip her boobies out to breast feed in public.

Yes, your friendship has changed, and so has your friend. That cool chick who used to ski drunk in the Alps and drive a Corvette now commutes in a minivan and finds fulfillment in changing diapers, heating bottles, and attending baby groups with other, equally annoying procreators.

It is time to get even with the woman who turned your happy twosome into a miserable threesome.

TOP FIVE THINGS YOU SHOULDN'T SAY TO A DEPRESSED FRIEND

① "Guess things really can't get worse."

② "Wow! You look like Hell."

③ "Glad I'm not you."

④ "Man, I'd just kill myself!"

⑤ "Cheer Up!"

FUN WAYS TO TORTURE THE ANNOYING NEW MOTHER

Of Curse I Can Help! Asked to babysit for the Thing while the Annoying New Mother runs some errands? No problem. Take this opportunity to teach the Thing how to curse. Once it has mastered four-letter words, it is really difficult to stop it from blurting them out in public. If possible, teach the Thing to curse right before the family has to attend a church or synagogue service.

Crack a Smile With some scissors, slice a few cracks in all of the Thing's bottles so that they leak all over the place.

Sorry You Can't Come Whenever the Annoying New Mother is stuck at home on a Friday night steaming the colic out of the snot-nosed Thing, swing by dressed to the nines and mention that you are on your way out to a wild party but "just wanted to say hi." Then wave ta-ta to her and the Thing as you step back into your rented limo filled with the male strippers.

Bourbon the Baby Next time you can convince the Annoying Mother to go shopping with you, she will inevitably bring the Thing along. So secretly dip its pacifier in bourbon and pop the pacifier back in its mouth. Yes, the Thing may eventually develop a dependency problem. But at least you'll get to finish shopping.

Is That Normal? Nothing makes the Annoying New Mother more paranoid than thinking her child is defective. So, point to the kid's perfectly normal eyes and gulp, "Wow, he really is a bit cross-eyed, isn't he?" Pick him up and say, "Is his head supposed to be this big?" Play with the Thing on the floor and casually remark, "I'm sure he'll catch up to the other babies eventually." The more imaginary flaws you draw attention to, the less inclined is the Annoying New Mother to show the Thing off.

Fisher Priceless Buy completely inappropriate baby gifts for the little bundle of joy. A power saw, rock candy, a set of marbles, a book of matches.

Booger Nights: Offer to help the Annoying New Mother prepare her birth announcement cards, complete with the usual nauseating "professional" portrait of the Thing sitting on some stool in front of a background of bubbles and teddy bears. While your friend is busy addressing the envelopes, take a green marker and add booger-like dots under the Thing's nose on all the photos. Then seal them up, address, stamp, and mail the suckers.

The Alum-lie Office: Call the alumni office of whatever college the Annoying New Mother graduated from and update her bio for the next alumni magazine as "unmarried, no children."

The Photo Op Never acknowledge any of the baby photos the Annoying New Mother insists on e-mailing you day in and day out. When she asks if you got them, respond with a flat "Yes." Then change the subject to something important like the weather.

Oh, Baby! Get a baby of your own. (Adopt, if you don't feel like going through labor.) The Annoying New Mother will resent the competition immensely.

• BRINGING OUT YOUR INNER SMART GIRL •

YOUR NEW SMART GIRL GAL PAL COMMANDMENTS

① *Support Her Like a Bra:* No matter how many acts of gal pal stupidity you witness, you must do all that you can to avoid passing judgment on your friends. Let the Bad Judgment Girl continue her affair with the married guy, and the Preachy Social Activist develop anemia due to lack of protein in her diet. For as difficult as it is to watch friends make foolish mistakes, they are their mistakes to make, and not yours to judge. And remind them of this philosophy when you do something stupid . . . which will, undoubtedly, be very soon.

② *Beeeeeep!* Never check your answering machine when a friend is visiting. Chances are pretty good that you have bitched about your guest to one of your other friends recently. And the last thing you need your guest to hear is a message like, "Hey, it's me. I can't believe you have to have dinner with that bitch-faced snob! Call me after she leaves and we'll make fun of her." There really isn't a graceful way out of that situation.

③ *Tell Her What She Wants to Hear:* When a gal pal asks you if she looks fat in her jeans, you may be perfectly justified in replying to the bulbous piece of lard, "Why yes! I nearly mistook you for a walrus!" But this would be wrong. Speaking the truth and, thereby, hurting your girlfriend's feelings will only put an unnecessary strain on an otherwise healthy friendship. If you must protect her from public embarrassment, candy-coat the criticism so it sounds like a compliment. "Well, they look great, but why not get a new pair that really shows off your great boobs a bit more?"

④ *The Benefit of the Doubt:* Just as you are bound to accidentally hurt a friend's feelings from time to time, your gal pals are likely to disappoint you once in a while as well. But, unless one of your girls runs you over with her car . . . on more than one occasion . . . or sells you into the sex trade without your permission, give her the benefit of the doubt when she fumbles a bit. If a gal pal forgets your birthday, resist the temptation to firebomb her house. Assume she just had something else on her mind and let it go for a few days. Then, when she finally catches her oversight, she'll feel compelled to spend twice as much on your birthday gift. See how it all works out in the end?

TOP FIVE REASONS TO HAVE AN UGLY FRIEND

① You'll always be the prettier one.

② The fatter she is, the thinner you look.

③ Compared to her, you never have a bad hair day.

④ You'll have one less Halloween mask to buy each year.

⑤ Your dog needs a playmate.

5 *The Confrontation:* Never, ever send an angry e-mail to a friend. No matter how right you are, no matter how wrong she is, if you need to confront her about a problem, do it in person. Not in writing. Facial expressions, vocal tones, and body language are very helpful when it comes to communicating your feelings. But the written word can be easily misinterpreted. And worse, it is permanent. The last thing you want is for you girls to kiss and make up only to have your gal pal come across your hate mail a year letter and rethink the friendship entirely. Right before your birthday nonetheless!

PART FOUR

The Family

Blood Is Thicker Than Water . . . and Pretty Much Any
Condiment Except Molasses

• • •

Ten Signs You're a Pushover with Your Family

1. You agree to host every Thanksgiving dinner at your place, on your dime.

2. You keep loaning your siblings money even though you can't pay your own bills.

3. You apologize to your mother for being related to her.

4. You only recognize family members when they are drunk.

5. Your home has become a motel for wayward relatives.

6. You spend more money on your niece and nephew than you do on yourself.

7. Your family is featured on *Jerry Springer.*

8. Your stepmother is younger than you.

9. Your father has scared off every boyfriend you've ever had.

10. You envy orphans.

Unlike a lousy gift, you cannot return bad relatives to the store and get your money back. Heck, you can't even exchange them for better relatives. Sadly, you were not afforded the opportunity to pick your family while killing time in the womb, and thereby are stuck with these people for the rest of your life. The nosey mother, the bitter sister, the can-do-no-wrong brother, the intoxicated aunt and uncle, the overprotective father, the evil stepmother. Like it or not, they are a part of you. Permanently attached to you FOREVER.

And there ain't nothing you can do to get rid of them . . . nothing legal at least. That means you have a lifetime of family feuds, expensive gift purchases, and intolerable holiday dinners through which to suffer. You had better get a little payback before these nut cases get the best of you.

CHAPTER 28

The Buttinsky Mother

(Latin: *Nooseus aroundus yer neckus*)

● OBSERVED BEHAVIOR IN NATURAL HABITAT ●

This creature eavesdrops on your phone calls, peeks through your diary, and inserts herself into every facet of your life, every moment of every day. She leaves forty messages on your answering machine daily and freaks out if you don't call her back forty times a day. She picked your date for the prom, your dress for the prom, and even knew you lost your virginity at the prom before you did. She has a comment for every hairstyle and outfit you wear, every boyfriend you bring home, every pound you put on or take off, every apartment you rent, and every job you lose. Basically, this woman could be on another continent entirely and still get on your nerves.

● OFTEN HEARD SAYING ●

"I don't mean to butt in, but . . ."

"Well, if you want my opinion . . ."

"Far be it from me to tell you what to do, but . . ."

"You paid for that haircut?"

"I only have your best interest at heart."

• WHY YOU MUST TAKE ACTION •

Privacy. It is not something you should have to move to Zimbabwe to obtain. But if you do not put the Buttinsky Mother in her place fast, her frightening ability to control your life may force you to take such Draconian measures. You are a grown woman and therefore entitled to live your life on your terms, not your mother's. If she wants a diary to read, let it be your fat sister's, right?

By exacting revenge in both small and big ways you have the power to make the Buttinsky Mother wish she never eavesdropped on your phone calls. Or read your e-mails. Or told you which guy to date. Or which hairstyle to wear. Freedom from the Buttinsky Mother is just a hop, skip, and minor legal infraction away. So, seize it.

Otherwise, you'll find yourself sharing some clay hut in Zimbabwe with a bunch of natives who wear elephant tusks pierced through their noses. And getting a wireless Internet connection in a clay hut is next to impossible.

• IT'S REVENGE TIME! •

With a few simple, but slightly vicious actions, you are going to teach the Buttinsky Mother to obey some boundaries, once and for all. You have the power to turn the Buttinsky Mother into the Butt*outs*ky Mother. And that means being able to wear your hair any way you darn well want to!

THE SUBTLE APPROACH

1. *You Have No Messages:* Toss your answering machine in the garbage and have your cellular phone service provider cancel your voice mail system. What the Buttinsky Mother can't leave in a message can't hurt you!

2. *Silence Is Golden:* Whenever you have to visit the Buttinsky Mother, pretend you have laryngitis. No matter how much she

nags, she won't be able to get any information out of you. And that means your life is entirely your own, if only until her next nightmare visit.

3 *Advice-a-Versa:* Whenever the Buttinsky Mother bombards you with her unwanted opinions of what she thinks you should do, thank her politely for her advice. Then do the exact opposite. If she suggests you grow your hair long, shave your head bald as a cue ball. If she wants you to date her best friend's son—the one with the law degree—date her best friend's other son . . . the one in prison. She thinks you should invest all your money in oil? Call your broker right away and tell him to buy stock in reversible toilet paper.

THE NOT-SO-SUBTLE APPROACH

1 *A Run in the Oven:* The Buttinsky Mother prides herself on knowing everything about you, even the last time you moved your bowels. So imagine how frustrated she will be when you show all signs of being pregnant, but refuse to acknowledge being "with child." Whenever you are visiting the Buttinsky Mother, excuse yourself to the bathroom every twelve minutes, nibble on pickles and ice cream, and complain about your upset tummy. Wear bulky clothing and waddle a lot. Maybe even ask the Buttinsky Mother what her favorite baby names are. Keep this up for nine months. Then repeat as necessary.

2 *The Coma Sutra:* Pretend you have slipped into a coma. This will be a terrible inconvenience to the Buttinsky Mother. It means she will have to forgo meeting her bridge club to sit by your hospital bedside day in and day out, and sell off those alligator shoes to pay for the exorbitant medical bills accrued by your perpetual state of vegetation. And she can forget that Caribbean cruise she's been planning for the fall; the only buffet snacks she'll be enjoying are whatever Jell-O remnants the nurse can't force down your feeding tube.

❸ *The Ted Bundy:* In your diary confess to the serial killings that have been making headlines in the local news. Then leave the diary open on your bed for her to read. Leave packing tape and loose piano wire around the house, too, for added effect. The Buttinsky Mother will be too afraid to ask you about your nocturnal activities, and will opt to keep her distance, lest you lose your temper with her.

THE YOU'RE GOING TO HELL APPROACH

❶ *The Ball Buster:* Within earshot of the Buttinsky Mother pick up the nearest phone extension and begin discussing the details of your impending sex-change operation. Whisper things like, "Will my testicles be functional?" and "How soon will my facial hair grow?" Then hang up the phone and tell the Buttinsky Mother it was just a wrong number.

❷ *Your Better Half:* They say that every human has a twin somewhere. So, find yours and pay her $12 an hour to play you at family affairs. Let her be the one to suffer the Buttinsky Mother's incessant nagging while you go hang out at the beach and work on your tan. You may feel the pinch of this new expense, but money truly can buy happiness!

❸ *Your Native Tongue:* Move to Zimbabwe. Yes, this will mean bathing in a river filled with piranha and dining on charbroiled rats. But you can rest assured that the Buttinsky Mother won't be using her frequent flyer miles to visit you over the summer.

• TOP THREE GIFTS TO GIVE THE BUTTINSKY MOTHER •

① Happy Mother's Day cards delivered COD.

② A coffee mug that reads, "Dads are the best!"

③ *Mommie Dearest* on DVD.

CHAPTER 29

The Highly Conservative, Religious, Overprotective Father

(Latin: *Paternus with shotgunus*)

• OBSERVED BEHAVIOR IN NATURAL HABITAT •

This creature is usually a registered conservative Republican who votes against any laws that give women, homosexuals, or poor people any rights. He carries a Bible and a 12-gauge shotgun with him at all times and believes that sex is the root of all evil. He sees everything in life as a hazard to his daughter's well-being, has scared off every boyfriend you've ever had, and has, on more than one occasion, complained that your winter parka is too revealing.

• OFTEN HEARD SAYING •

"Lipstick is the Devil's makeup."

"Let us pray."

"I just need to take a sample of your DNA."

"You'll always be Daddy's little girl."

"Have my daughter home by midnight or I'll gut you like a fish."

• WHY YOU MUST TAKE ACTION •

With his brass knuckles, 12-gauge shotgun, and Bible in hand, the Highly Conservative, Religious, Overprotective Father controls way too much of your life. But it is no longer his business whom you date, what you wear, or where you go. You are a grown woman. Yes, it is possible that your father is correct about your burning in Hell for wearing thong underwear. But if you want to burn in Hell, that is your choice, not his. Don't let the Highly Conservative, Religious, Overprotective Father force his beliefs on you . . . or your underwear for that matter.

• IT'S REVENGE TIME! •

The Highly Conservative, Religious, Overprotective Father assumes that because he was part of your creation, he is forever part of your life. Show him that you and he believe in very different things. And that Almighty God ain't the only one who gets angry!

THE SUBTLE APPROACH

1 *Epiphany #1:* Hide the Highly Conservative, Religious, Overprotective Father's Bible. He will spend the time he would usually devote to lecturing you on the evils of sex and television searching high and low for the word of God. That gives you more time to, well, have sex and watch television.

2 *Dad, I'd Like You to Meet . . .* Embark on a romance with a serial killer on Death Row who has tattoos covering 90 percent of his body.

3 *Vote for the Elephant:* Become a registered Democrat. That'll damn near kill the Highly Conservative, Religious, Overprotective Father.

THE NOT-SO-SUBTLE APPROACH

❶ *Epiphany #2:* The Highly Conservative, Religious, Over-protective Father has devoted his entire life to serving God, and imposing his beliefs on you. So, hit him where it hurts. Convert to another religion entirely. And invite him to the conversion ceremony!

❷ *Saint Chick Pea:* Tell your father that you have had a very religious experience. God came to you in the middle of the night in the form of a chick pea. Begin worshipping chick peas. Crucify a chick pea to a piece of plywood and pray to it day and night. Carry a photo of Saint Chick Pea in your wallet. Scream and throw Holy Water whenever a family member eats a chick pea with his/her salad at the dinner table. The Highly Conservative, Religious, Overprotective Father will wish you had never seen "the way."

❸ *Turning Tricks:* On the next family trip, while staying at whatever flea bag motel the Highly Conservative, Religious, Overprotective Father has forced you to stay in, pay some local teenage boys to knock on your door every hour on the hour and enter your room for about forty-five minutes. Then have them exit your room, with their hair all messed up and their clothing on backward. The Highly Conservative, Religious, Overprotective Father will not be able to sleep knowing such "acts of deviance" are being performed by his daughter. And that means he won't have the energy in the morning to drag you to the Museum of Republican Propaganda.

THE YOU'RE GOING TO HELL APPROACH

❶ *Epiphany #3:* Become an atheist. Nothing pisses off a religious zealot more than someone who believes in nothing. Someone who doesn't kneel and pray, stand and pray, kneel, then stand, then kneel, then bow, then pray. Forsake all that is religious and scream whenever you see the Bible.

❷ *Homo Sweet Homo:* Throw the Highly Conservative, Religious, Overprotective Father's next surprise birthday party at a gay bar, Your Bible-carrying pa will be especially self-conscious when you tell him to "blow" out the candles in front of all the drag queens dressed like Bette Midler.

❸ *La Cage aux Faux:* The Highly Conservative, Religious, Overprotective Father is very proud of the religious beliefs he has imposed on you. And he will inevitably invite all of his church congregation over to watch old home movies of you being baptized, confirmed, taking your first Communion, and so forth. What the Highly Conservative, Religious, Overprotective Father doesn't know is that you've replaced the old family videos with a raunchy porno tape.

• TOP THREE GIFTS TO GIVE THE HIGHLY CONSERVATIVE, RELIGIOUS, OVERPROTECTIVE FATHER •

❶ Madonna's "Like a Prayer" video.

❷ A membership to an underground sex club.

❸ A framed photograph of Charles Manson.

CHAPTER 30

The Jealous and Vindictive Older Sister

(Latin: *Cain-us and abel-us*)

• OBSERVED BEHAVIOR IN NATURAL HABITAT •

This creature is the first born. The forgotten child of the family. The off-spring on which your folks practiced and thereby made some really regret-table mistakes with. Unfortunately, *you* are now paying for those mistakes, for the Jealous and Vindictive Older Sister holds you personally responsi-ble for her misery. She shoots daggers at you across the dinner table at family gatherings, seething with the memories of Saturday nights she spent babysitting you when she could have been getting to second base with her boyfriend. Of how she was forced to go to the lesser college so that you, the younger and cuter one, could go to the better school. She be-lieves your existence is the root of all her failures in life, and sabotages you every chance she gets. From deliberately excluding you from family affairs and refusing to acknowledge your birthday to poisoning the minds of other relatives against you, every bitter word she utters, every underhanded ac-tion she takes is intended to make you pay for not being born first.

• OFTEN HEARD SAYING •

"You've always had it so easy."

"DIE, BITCH! DIE!"

"Oh, I didn't know YOU were going to be here."

"You were always Mom and Dad's favorite."

"Bitter? Me? I'm not bitter."

● WHY YOU MUST TAKE ACTION ●

It's not your fault that the Jealous and Vindictive Older Sister got the short end of the stick. True, you always got to sit on Santa's lap at the mall for the holiday family photo while she got tucked behind the elf. And if we must be honest, yes, you always got the bigger ice cream sundae for dessert and the front seat in the car. But that doesn't give her the right to make your life miserable, does it? No. And it most certainly doesn't give her the right to try and kill you.

● IT'S REVENGE TIME! ●

Nothing is more entertaining than watching an already jealous woman get more jealous. So, sit back, relax, and enjoy the show!

THE SUBTLE APPROACH

❶ *The Silver Scream:* When the Jealous and Vindictive Older Sister is in a particularly foul mood, pass on a few pick-me-up movies to her: *Schindler's List, Titanic, Brian's Song, Love Story, Old Yeller.* When she confronts you, in tears, to accuse you of exploiting her suicidal tendencies, respond with a puzzled look on your face. "What are you talking about? Those are hilarious comedies! You must be reading something into them."

❷ *Five Al-arm Candy:* Bring along a brutally handsome date to every family event. Rent a boyfriend from a male escort service if you have to. Just do whatever it takes to arrive at every family function with major arm candy. Then spend the whole time making out with him. Oh, and talking about the Pulitzer Prize you just won.

❸ *Get Well Soon:* Once a week mail a "Get Well" card to the Jealous and Vindictive Older Sister. This will confuse her, because she hasn't been sick.

THE NOT-SO-SUBTLE APPROACH

❶ *The Photo Op:* Next time you are at your folks' house, sneak into the den with a pair of scissors and cut out the Jealous and Vindictive Older Sister's face from every single family photo. The annual holiday group shots, her baby photos, her graduation picture—pretty funny considering she's the only one in that photo! If she didn't feel a part of the family already, imagine how she'll feel now!

❷ *Party of One?* Before the Jealous and Vindictive Older Sister arrives for Thanksgiving, make sure to set two place settings for her—one for her, and the other for the date she will never bring. The extra knife, fork, spoon, salad plate, entrée plate, and champagne glass to her left will be a constant reminder to her fat face that she has no one. When she gripes about being seated next to an imaginary date, feign embarrassment and remark with an innocent shrug, "Oh, silly! I just assumed you were bringing someone . . . this time." See, there is more than one turkey getting roasted this holiday season!

❸ *And the Winner Is:* Anonymously enter the Jealous and Vindictive Older Sister into the Westminster Dog Show. She'll probably win, too!

THE YOU'RE GOING TO HELL APPROACH

❶ *Trick or Treat:* Every time the Jealous and Vindictive Older Sister shows up for a family event, point to her face and say, "Hey, cool Halloween mask!" When she explains that she is not wearing a mask, act all embarrassed and change the subject to the weather. She'll spend the rest of the night locked in the bathroom crying into the soap dish. And that means you can enjoy a few hours of happiness sans her vexing presence.

② *Recipe for Revenge:* Whenever the Jealous and Vindictive Older Sister worms her way over for dinner, take this opportunity to crush some Prozac in the kitchen while she's sulking in the living room. Then sprinkle the antidepressant dust onto her food and dinner is served! Thanks to the wonder of drugs she'll be the most pleasant of company all the way through dessert. And if you're real lucky she will overdose and slip into a temporary coma. Yay! More cheesecake for you!

③ *The Last Will and Testament:* "Accidentally" forward to the Jealous and Vindictive Older Sister a fake postcard from your parents. "Dear favorite daughter, wishing you were here. We love you the most. How could we not? You're not the adopted one! You get everything when we die. Love Mom and Dad."

• TOP THREE GIFTS TO GIVE THE JEALOUS AND VINDICTIVE OLDER SISTER •

① A jar of cyanide chewables.

② Fourteen cats and a housecoat.

③ A noose.

CHAPTER 31

The Favorite Son

(Latin: *Thornus in your sideus*)

• OBSERVED BEHAVIOR IN NATURAL HABITAT •

Ever since being voted Valedictorian in nursery school, this creature has been making your life miserable. His boyhood room was filled with awards for excellence in sports, academics, drama, and even space flight, while the best you could muster up as a kid was the award for "Most Mediocre Student in the Special Ed Class." The Favorite Son always got the biggest allowance, the front seat on family road trips, the biggest birthday present, the ice cream sundae with the most whipped cream. Meanwhile, you got stuck with the hand-me-down clothing and used toothbrushes. And still, today, your parents' home is plastered with framed photographs of their prized offspring, while you're lucky if they even remember your name.

• OFTEN HEARD SAYING •

"Mom and Dad love me most."

"Did you see my Olympic Gold Medal?"

"I read *Ulysses* just for fun."

"Oh, Harvard was just my safety school."

"I'm spending my vacation feeding the homeless in Uganda. You?"

• WHY YOU MUST TAKE ACTION •

Your parents aren't getting any younger. But they are getting richer. And the longer the Favorite Son remains their offspring of choice, the farther away slip your chances of getting a good inheritance. You must ingratiate yourself to your parents immediately. Or else, come inheritance time, you will watch the Favorite Son drive away in your Ferrari.

• IT'S REVENGE TIME! •

By making the Favorite Son not so much of a family favorite anymore, you will look all the better! Turn him into the shame of the family. For then, and only then, will the Favorite Son know what it is like to be you.

THE SUBTLE APPROACH

1. *Happy Holidaze # 1:* During the holiday season, sneak under the tree while the Favorite Son is in the bathroom. Any of his wrapped packages for Mom and Dad that look breakable? Well, drop those babies on the floor a few times. Then place them back under the tree.

2. *Handicapped Parking:* Break the legs off of all the figures on the Favorite Son's athletic awards. "Best Short Distance Sprinter," "Hockey MVP," "Best Male Ballerina."

3. *Map Inquest:* The next time the family has to gather at an auditorium to watch the Favorite Son receive yet another award for perfection, secretly program your father's GPS unit to follow directions that go by way of say, Guadalahara. By the time you all arrive, only the folding chairs will be left in the auditorium.

THE NOT-SO-SUBTLE APPROACH

1. *Happy Holidaze # 2:* Take whatever fancy gifts the Favorite Son puts under the holiday tree for your parents, cross out his name

on the name tag and replace it with yours. Mom and Dad will realize how much they underestimated you when they open the beautiful pearl necklace and fancy tool kit you gave them. Not to mention seriously reevaluate their misdirected affection for the Favorite Son, who gave them some used CDs and a pencil sharpener.

② *The Discourtesy Flush:* Every time you are at your folks' home, wait until the Favorite Son has to use the bathroom. Once he has exited the lavatory, sneak in and drop a giant pile of dog poop into the toilet bowl. Don't flush. Instead, turn up the heat on the thermostat to the highest level and run away.

③ *It's Snot Me, It's You.* Never tell the Favorite Son when he has a booger hanging from his nose. No one likes a booger head. No one.

THE YOU'RE GOING TO HELL APPROACH

① *Happy Holidaze #3:* The Favorite Son won't be such a favorite after you secretly replace the diamond bracelet he plans to present to Mom on Mother's Day with a giant dildo. And Dad sure won't be laughing when he gets the same thing for Father's Day.

② *The Testy-Monial:* When the local news station interviews you for a few comments on what it is like being related to the brave man who saved fourteen children from a burning school bus, respond on camera with the following, "Oh, I am so proud of him. Especially because he's gotten over his heroin addiction."

③ *While You Were Sleeping:* Kill the Favorite Son in his sleep and make it look like a suicide.

• TOP THREE GIFTS TO GIVE THE FAVORITE SON •

1. A mug with his picture on it that says, "We Hate You."

2. A burial plot . . . in Uganda.

3. A picture of a giant ass with lips on it.

CHAPTER 32

The Bratty Little Nephew

(Latin: *Menace extraordinairus*)

● OBSERVED BEHAVIOR IN NATURAL HABITAT ●

This creature stands about three feet tall, but holds more power in his tiny, snot-filled palm than all the other family members combined. He is a constant fixture at every family function—running, screaming, pulling at your clothes, crying, picking his nose, and making farting noises whenever you move in your chair. He amuses himself by kicking the door open when you are doing something disgusting in the bathroom, or making you play Hide & Seek for hours at a clip. And he communicates not through words, but via bites, wails, and tantrums. . . . Not unlike many of your ex-boyfriends.

● OFTEN HEARD SAYING ●

"Pick me up! Pick me up!"

"Let's play Hide & Seek. You're It!"

"I WANT . . ."

"Mommy says you have to . . ."

"Auntie, what's this rubber thing in your purse?"

● WHY YOU MUST TAKE ACTION ●

If you wanted to spend all your free time at family affairs fending off the attacks of a horrid little buck-toothed terror on two feet, you would have had a son of your own, right? You had nothing to do with the inception of the Bratty Little Nephew, and yet, you are expected to fawn all over him, entertain him, and spend your hard-earned money on him. How much longer are you going to allow this Baby Gap–clad, vertically challenged monster to steal the tampons out of your purse, soak them in water, and then sling shot them across the room at your head? And you don't even want to THINK about how much this creature will cost you over the years in gifts.

● IT'S REVENGE TIME! ●

Like that not-so-hot stock tip your brother gave you that left you nearly broke, the Bratty Little Nephew is a bad investment . . . and one that was forced on you at that. For all the money and time you invest in this child of Satan, you have nothing to show for it but an empty wallet and spaghetti sauce splattered across your silk blouse. For the sake of victimized aunts and uncles worldwide, take back your life, woman! Pull rank on this rug rat.

THE SUBTLE APPROACH

1. *Pucker Up:* Force sloppy, wet kisses on the Bratty Little Nephew. Children hate, hate, HATE being kissed. Even more than they hate Brussels sprouts. So, smooch away! Any time the little monster is within arm's reach, slap a few smackaroos all over his face. Oh, and make sure to squeeze his cheeks a lot, too. It won't be long before the Bratty Little Nephew is avoiding you at all costs.

2. *You've Got Stain Power:* Spray a layer of Scotch Guard stain resistant coating over the outfit you are wearing to the next fam-

ily function. Whatever meat sauce or cranberry juice the Bratty Little Nephew hurls in your general direction, you can rest assured it won't do much damage. Can't say the same for his outfit, now can he? Hee-hee.

❸ *Cut to the Chase:* Under the guise of an Auntly bonding session, take the Bratty Little Nephew into the nearest bathroom and give him a new haircut with a butter knife. It will be months before Mommy and Daddy will have the nerve to take him out in public.

THE NOT-SO-SUBTLE APPROACH

❶ *Biological Warfare:* When no one else is listening, whisper to the Bratty Little Nephew, "Pssst. Did you know that Mommy and Daddy aren't your real mommy and daddy?" Then smile widely, pat the creature on the head, and walk away. Surprisingly, comments like that have a way of sticking in a child's brain . . . even with lots of expensive therapy sessions.

❷ *The Ex Con:* The next time you have to schlep to another stupid birthday party for the Bratty Little Nephew (man, they seem to come like, once every year!) bring along your new boyfriend: a registered sex offender. This will pretty much guarantee you won't have to attend any more parties in the little monster's honor for a long time. Apparently, parents don't "feel comfortable" letting their kids play Pin the Tail on the Donkey with child molesters. Waaaaaaaaaa!

❸ *Scout's Dishonor:* Make some easy cash at the Bratty Little Nephew's expense, the next time he bullies you into buying those insipid cookies he's hocking to raise money for a school trip. Agree to buy, say, six boxes. Then pay for the cookies with a dollar bill and tell the Bratty Little Nephew that you are owed

$20 in change. Let's face it, the kid eats boogers—he's definitely too stupid to count. Pocket the $19 profit and use it to buy some cookies that don't taste like poop.

THE YOU'RE GOING TO HELL APPROACH

❶ *The Speaker System:* Like all children, the Bratty Little Nephew is a walking megaphone. So if you want information disseminated quickly and loudly, use the little monster to get your message across. While the rest of the family is busy catching up at the dinner table, whisper a deep, dark secret into the ear of the Bratty Little Nephew. Like about the time your sister got really drunk and had a threesome with Father O'Reilly and Rabbi Sheinstein. It will be but a few precious moments until the Bratty Little Nephew will blurt out in front of everyone, "Mommy, why did you have sex with the priest and the rabbi?" Talk about a spanking!

❷ *The Classic Switcheroo:* Whenever you have to visit your sister and her loathsome child, take whatever private time you can get in the house to make some changes to the kid's DVD collection. Secretly remove the SpongeBob DVDs and replace them with *The Exorcist,* Parts I, II, and III. The *Thomas the Train* DVD series with *Jaws,* Parts I, II, III, IV, & XXVII. *Beauty and the Beast* with *Debbie Does Dallas.* Like most mothers your sister is too busy cleaning up spilled milk, sorting laundry, and scheduling play dates to actually look at that DVD she just popped into the player for Junior to watch.

❸ *In the Dog House:* As a special gift to the Bratty Little Nephew, bring home a full-grown, abused pit bull. You know, the kind of dog with a head as big as a horse's and a hatred for all things human. The Bratty Little Nephew will give Fido something really tasty to sink his three-inch-long fangs into.

● TOP THREE GIFTS TO GIVE THE BRATTY LITTLE NEPHEW ●

1 A cactus planted in the Bratty Little Nephew's honor.

2 Socks and underwear.

3 Books in a foreign language.

CHAPTER 33

The Evil Stepmother

(Latin: *Satan in pantyhoseus*)

● **OBSERVED BEHAVIOR IN NATURAL HABITAT** ●

With her perfectly coiffed hair and manicured nails, this creature has slowly, but surely, squirmed her way into your father's life and pushed you out of it. Cold and calculating, she has chipped away at the man your father used to be, transforming him into someone you scarcely recognize—the mere shell of the man you idolized when your mother was married to him. The dad to whom you once felt so close . . . the guy who wore corduroys year-round and drove a beat-up Volkswagen Beetle now dresses in Abercrombie and Fitch, drives a convertible, and highlights his hair. All because the Evil Stepmother wants him to! This bitch refuses to acknowledge your mother's existence at all, and barely tolerates your presence at family affairs. She conveniently "forgets" to pass on your phone messages to your father and only includes you in family affairs when she is forced to. In short, she sucks.

● **OFTEN HEARD SAYING** ●

"No, you cannot go to the ball with your stepsisters."

"I'm pretty sure I gave my husband your message."

"Your father was very unhappy with his old life."

"We're just having immediate family over for the holidays."

"Now, about that will . . ."

• WHY YOU MUST TAKE ACTION •

Despite the fact that your parents' nuptials didn't work out, the bond between a father and daughter should never be broken, especially by some high heel–wearing devil woman. The Evil Stepmother may have walked off with what should have been your mother's happy marriage, but you sure as heck can't let her walk off with your father as well! This is the man who is duty-bound to give you a hug on a bad day, advice on a boyfriend, or an oil change for your car! Don't allow the Evil Stepmother to get in the way of those most lovely father-daughter moments . . . they are your birthright. Besides, you don't know a thing about changing oil!

• IT'S REVENGE TIME! •

More than anything the Evil Stepmother fears her husband's past. She is threatened by anything and everything that singals her husband had a life before her. As long as his ex-wife and children are in the picture, this woman fails to have complete control. See where we're going with this?

THE SUBTLE APPROACH

❶ *Once Upon a Time:* Every time you get the Evil Stepmother on the phone when calling to speak with your father, introduce yourself as Cinderella. It's subtle, but she's probably smart enough to get it.

❷ *Till Death Do Us Part:* Keep leaving your mother's wedding photo album at the Evil Stepmother's house. Like on her bed.

❸ *Who's Your Mommy?* Gain access to the Evil Stepmother's house phone. She will inevitably have her evil children on her speed dial. Delete their numbers and replace them with your mother's phone number instead. Every time the Evil Stepmother attempts to call her children, she'll have to field a more than awkward phone call with her hubby's ex.

THE NOT-SO-SUBTLE APPROACH

1. *Beat Her to the Punch:* Under the guise of extending an olive branch of sorts, offer to join the Evil Stepmother on a shopping errand. Return from the excursion with a fake black eye and some bruises on your neck. When your father asks what happened, nod your head toward the Evil Stepmother and shake your head and whisper, "I'll be fine, Daddy. Really." Then limp away, weeping into your sleeve.

2. *Tilt for Tat:* Shave down the heel of one shoe in every pair of high-heels the Evil Stepmother has in her closet. She'll spend the entire day trying to figure out why she's slanting to one side when she walks.

3. *Downsizing:* Buy the Evil Stepmother a cashmere sweater for her birthday—but in a child's size. Then change the label to read Adult Size 10. When she opens it, insist that she try it on in front of everyone. She'll be suffering from anorexia before you know it! And the less there is of her, the less there is to get on your nerves.

THE YOU'RE GOING to HELL APPROACH

1. *Up and Coming:* Secretly replace your father's supply of Viagra with garlic tablets. Not only will he suffer from erectile dysfunction and the embarrassment thereafter, but he'll stink to high heavens. Won't be long before Pa's sleeping on the couch.

2. *Botoxic Shock Syndrome:* While she is sleeping, secretly inject Botox into the Evil Stepmother's forehead. This will make it im-

possible for her to look anything but entirely thrilled by your company at all times. No matter how much she hates you, she will not be able to show it. And that will frustrate her to no end.

③ *Check, Please:* Whenever the Evil Stepmother is hosting an affair to which you were not invited, show up anyway and do a little damage to her catering. Walk around the dishes she has set along the table and dump handfuls of salt into each, including the desserts. She will be the hostess with the leastess . . . and even the most loyal of the family brood won't be able to stick up for her, what with all the vomiting they'll be doing in the guest room.

• TOP THREE GIFTS TO GIVE THE EVIL STEPMOTHER •

① A glass slipper that doesn't fit her foot.

② A rotten pumpkin.

③ A boa . . . constrictor that hasn't eaten in a year.

CHAPTER 34

The Deadbeat Dad

(Latin: Trailer parkus ratus)

• OBSERVED BEHAVIOR IN NATURAL HABITAT •

Like the single sock that mysteriously disappears every time you do a load of laundry, this creature has been missing in action most of your life. Countless holidays have floated on by without so much as a card from him, and he sure as heck didn't help you with college tuition or boyfriend troubles. He calls about once a year to wish you a Happy Birthday, but inevitably has the date wrong. He never taught you how to drive a car, put up dry wall, or choose a draft beer. And what's worse? He has no shame about it!

• OFTEN HEARD SAYING •

(Nothing . . . you haven't heard from him in years.)

• WHY YOU MUST TAKE ACTION •

The minute your screaming infant face came into the picture at the hospital, the Deadbeat Dad was out the door faster than the doctor could say, "It's a girl!" Not only did this loser leave your mother to raise you single-handedly, but even now, when you're all grown up, he knows nothing about you or the woman you have become. You deserve to have a father in your life . . . because who else are you gonna hit up for money, right?

• IT'S REVENGE TIME! •

The Deadbeat Dad owes you quality time and money. Get both back—tenfold.

THE SUBTLE APPROACH

❶ *The Delicate Cycle:* Sneak into the Deadbeat Dad's home and steal all his clothes out of his "closet" (i.e., the chair closest to the television). Dump all his shirts into the washing machine, but add some red food coloring to the water. Then toss the newly pink duds into the dryer until they have shrunken three sizes. Return his clothes to his "closet" (i.e., the chair closest to the television).

❷ *The Belated Birthday Bill:* Count all the years you have been alive. Take this number and multiply it by 50. The total you come out with is what the Deadbeat Dad owes you in belated birthday gifts. Hand him a bill for said amount and give him until the end of the year to come through with the cash (gift certificates are acceptable). If the deadline is not met, you will report his lazy ass to the IRS.

❸ *The Con-Corder:* Make the Deadbeat Dad sit through hours and hours of home video footage of your life. From the moment you popped out of your mother's vagina to the recent video of you having a mole removed at the dermatologist's office. Trust us, that's torture. Real torture.

THE NOT-SO-SUBTLE APPROACH

❶ *Happy Trails to You* (perfect for the white trash Deadbeat Dad): In the middle of the night, as the Deadbeat Dad lies on his couch in a drunken stupor, roll his trailer to another location. Nothing is more frustrating than waking up and not knowing where you are.

❷ *Home Sweet Home:* Show up on the Deadbeat Dad's doorstep and announce that you are moving in. Tell him that you are just aching to catch up after all these years. Bring along the forty-six stray dogs you picked up at the pound as well.

❸ *The Birds and the Bees:* Regardless of how many men you have already bedded (you hussy!), tie the Deadbeat Dad to a chair and make him give you the Birds and the Bees talk. Talking about sex with your daughter is never comfortable. But talking about sex with your grown daughter who hates every cell of your being is even more uncomfortable.

THE YOU'RE GOING TO HELL APPROACH

❶ *All's Welfare in Love and War:* Contact the Social Security office on the Deadbeat Dad's behalf and inform them of his "sudden and unfortunate passing." Those government checks will stop rolling in almost immediately.

❷ *A Night at the Oprah:* Go off to Hollywood and become a famous actress. Make millions of dollars. Then go on *Oprah* and talk about how awful your father is. Make sure to say his full name on camera several times, maybe even give out his home address. He'll become the shame of the nation. And you? Well, Oprah will feel so badly for you she'll invite you to spend the weekend at her mansion!

❸ *Baby Him:* Borrow a bunch of babies from the local orphanage. Dump them all off at the Deadbeat Dad's trailer for the afternoon, promising you just need to run an errand and will be right back. Come back about a month later.

• TOP THREE GIFTS TO GIVE THE DEADBEAT DAD •

1 A job.

2 A second job.

3 A third job.

CHAPTER 35

The Alcoholic Aunt and Uncle

(Latin: AA-*us*)

● OBSERVED BEHAVIOR IN NATURAL HABITAT ●

They stumble into every family affair clutching the walls to keep themselves upright, burping and hiccupping their way through the evening. They stink of the mouthwash they guzzle, thinking it will disguise the fact they just sucked down a gallon of Jack Daniels. They accidentally give you someone else's gifts because they were drunk when they wrote out the gift tags. They talk too loud, breathe too heavily, refer to you as their nephew, and pass the gravy when you ask for the broccoli.

● OFTEN HEARD SAYING ●

"Give me one for the road."

"Who are you?"

"Flask? This isn't a flask. This is a . . . er . . . um, silver water bottle thing."

"Where am I?"

"I'll drive you home."

• WHY YOU MUST TAKE ACTION •

Being related to drunks is exhausting. It means you are always helping someone get dressed or undressed, or breaking up a fight or bailing someone out of jail. It means having to repeat your name all the time and get hugged by someone who smells like they bathed in Grey Goose. Not to mention the fact that drunks cannot remember anything—so forget about receiving a thank-you card for that nice party you threw in their honor. . . . They don't remember going to a party last night! . . . Heck, they don't even remember what happened five minutes ago!

• IT'S REVENGE TIME! •

The more insufferable you make the consequences of their drinking habit, the less inclined the Alcoholic Aunt and Uncle will be to attend family functions. And that's a good thing . . . a very good thing.

THE SUBTLE APPROACH

1. *The Bad Hangover #1:* Just as the Alcoholic Aunt and Uncle are leaving your parents' house, plant a few pieces of your mother's antique silverware into their coat pockets. Eventually, your mother will be down by an entire place setting—and the Alcoholic Aunt and Uncle won't be welcome quite so often at dinner.

2. *The Gift of Nothing:* Need to present the Alcoholic Aunt and Uncle with a gift? Simply take an empty box and gussy it all up with fancy paper and ribbons and bows. Wait until they are loaded up on liquor, then present it to them. When they sober up in the morning and see an empty box, they'll just assume they lost their gift in their drunken stupor. Get something for yourself with the money you saved!

3. *An Ungraceful Exit:* Change all the signs on local businesses in the neighborhood to read the opposite of what they should. All

"Push" doors will now have "Pull" signs on them and vice versa. Then watch the Alcoholic Aunt and Uncle struggle to get in and out of every shop. And they thought driving drunk was hard!

THE NOT-SO-SUBTLE APPROACH

1. *The Bad Hangover #2:* The next time the Alcoholic Aunt and Uncle pass out, undress them and drag their naked bodies on the lawn right before daybreak. They will sleep straight through sunrise . . . and wake up with one heck of an awful sunburn.

2. *Address the Issue:* Change the name on the street sign where you live. The Alcoholic Aunt and Uncle will drive in circles for hours trying to figure out why you moved without telling them.

3. *H_2O No!* Whenever the Alcoholic Aunt and Uncle come to a family function, water down any and all drinks they are slamming back. Not only will they find it impossible to get drunk, but they'll inadvertently end up spending most of the evening in the restroom from drinking all that water. And that's one time you don't have to play designated driver!

THE YOU'RE GOING TO HELL APPROACH

1. *The Bad Hangover #3:* Whenever the Alcoholic Aunt and Uncle are too intoxicated to drive themselves home, offer to give them a ride. To Hell that is! Drive them to the nearest ghetto and dump their passed-out selves onto the street. Then lay a sign across their bodies that reads, "We're Filthy Rich and Stinkin' Drunk." Yes, there is a slight chance they will be murdered by an angry mob because of your little prank. But at least you'll get your point across.

2. *Tomb-orrow Is Another Day:* Call the Alcoholic Aunt and Uncle to inform them of a death in the family. Give them the

address for a local cemetery and service information on the same date of the next family affair. They'll spend the day graveside, mourning the loss of a complete stranger and embarrassing someone else's family for a change.

❸ *Hi, My Name Is:* Sign them up for an Alcoholics Anonymous meeting at the local church and offer to drive them there.

• TOP THREE GIFTS TO GIVE THE ALCOHOLIC AUNT AND UNCLE •

❶ Matching flasks with matching holes in them.

❷ Ernest Hemmingway's biography.

❸ Breath mints.

CHAPTER 36

Smart Girl Tricks of the Trade

Getting Even by Getting Over

• HOW TO ENTERTAIN YOURSELF WHILE VISITING THE SENILE GRANDPARENTS AT THE NURSING HOME •

Senile Grandparents. They slip under the radar because they're supposedly "cute." But you know better. Senile Grandparents are nothing but annoying. You are sick and tired of having to give up weekends to visit them, hear them slurp strained peas through a straw, and knit pot holders that you'll never use. Watch the nurse give them sponge baths or listen to them talk to their imaginary friends. Ugh.

Well, if you must spend time with the old folks, at least make it a little entertaining for yourself, right?

1. Loosen the handicapped rails in all the nursing home bathrooms.

2. Switch your family for another one. That's the great thing about Alzheimer's. The Senile Grandparents won't know the difference.

3. Make a few changes to their will. Like, you inherit everything including the Swiss off-shore bank accounts Grandpa has that no one else knows about. Then get them to sign the new will

right after the nurse has come around with a double dose of their meds.

④ Cheat at nursing home Bingo games so that you win every time. Old people take Bingo very seriously.

⑤ Hide all the glitter from their arts and crafts boxes so they have nothing but chocolate chips to glue. Then tell them to leave the projects drying in the sun. You can be pretty sure you won't get another stupid pot holder from them for your birthday.

⑥ Change the dosages on all the patients' medical charts. Give this one too much Valium, and that one too little prednisone. It's fun to watch people bounce off the walls and slip in and out of vegetative states.

⑦ Add a finger of vodka to their Jell-O cups.

⑧ Start a game of Hide the Dentures.

⑨ Sew Grandma and Grandpa to their bed sheets.

⑩ Run up and down the halls screaming "Code Blue!"

• HOW TO FIGHT WITH YOUR MOTHER •

Except for whatever the heck that creepy thing going on between Hamlet and his mother was, there is no more complicated relationship than that between mother and daughter. Dealing with the Mother is hard work and exhausting. She makes you want to hug her and bite her. She is simultaneously your biggest critic and your most loyal fan; your best friend and your worst enemy; your therapist and the person who landed you in therapy. (And trust us, you are no picnic in the park for her, either!)

But since most mothers and daughters spend their time bickering, you must bone up on some of your fighting skills. The Mother is a worthy adversary and tough to beat. So follow these simple steps to gain some leverage:

1. *The Laundry List:* Like elephants, the Mother remembers everything. Her mind is a veritable Rolodex of filed ammunition—everything you have done wrong she remembers and stores away for future use. You must do the same. When you feel a fight coming on, take out a pad of paper and pen and jot down all the things the Mother has done wrong in the last twenty years. From that time she failed to buy you a tricycle for your fifth birthday to her getting drunk at your graduation, make note of every wrong move she has made. Then, just when she is preparing to launch into that "Don't you speak to me with that tone, Missy! I am your mother!" speech, rattle off everything on your list. The Mother will be so dumbstruck that you are still holding a grudge because she used generic brand disposable diapers, she will completely lose her train of thought. And that gives you time to come up with a really good excuse for why you forgot Mother's Day.

2. *The Bad Connection:* Nothing annoys the Mother more than the call-waiting feature on your phone. The Mother does not like being made to wait while your friend tells you what kinds of shoes she just bought on sale. So, whenever you are having a phone fight with the Mother, take every single incoming call-waiting call and leave her on hold for minutes at a time. This will cause her to lose focus. Do this several times. Then, for the final insult, return to her call and say, "Sorry, Mom, but I have another call. Hold on one second . . ." Then hang up. After the tenth time or so, the Mother will assume you got disconnected and give up for at least a few hours. And that, Smart Girl, gives you enough time to race to the airport and flee the country. (Note: If you don't have any friends who can be counted on to

call at the right time, simply press the "0" key on your phone's keypad with your chin. This will make a beeping noise similar to the call-waiting sound.)

③ *It's Snot Fair:* Contract a really disgusting strain of the flu. The Mother will not want to be around you, or even talk to you for that matter, if you are sniffling, sneezing, coughing, wheezing, hocking up phlegm. Get sick about once a month, and you'll be good to go for some peace and quiet.

④ *The Wrong Number:* Whenever you have done something really, really bad, and know the Mother is on the war path as a result of your stupidity, simply answer your phone with a Chinese accent. When she asks for her daughter, reply, "Yew haf wong numba!" Then hang up.

⑤ *The Death Knell:* If you feel yourself losing serious footing in a fight with the Mother, wait until she has seemingly won the fight and then blurt out, "I'M DYING!" This sort of makes whatever bone she was picking with you seem insignificant.

DISCLAIMER: Let's get something very clear. You are NEVER going to actually win a fight with the Mother. It is impossible. Mothers always win in the end. As a matter of fact, you stand a better chance getting struck by lightning—twice—than winning a fight with your mom. But at least you can give her a run for her money.

● HOW TO DRIVE AWAY THE UNWANTED HOUSE GUEST ●

One of the worst things about being part of a family is that your relatives assume they can visit you any time they feel like it and that you *want* them using your home as a hotel. "Hi! We're in town for a few nights and thought it would be fun to stay with you!" That sort of thing. So, when you find yourself the unwilling host to a party of annoying overnight guests, employ some of these choice tricks of the trade to shorten their stay. You won't have to worry about them visiting again for a very long time.

1. *Flush 'em Out:* If your overnight guests made the mistake of assuming your plumbing works, they'll be sorely disappointed. Clog the toilet with rotten avocados and remove all the toilet paper from the dispensers. When they ask where they can go to move their bowels, point to the shed in the backyard.

2. *The Leaning Towel of Pisa:* Apply a thin coat of industrial-strength glue to all of the bathroom towels. This will result in some nasty facial scratches whenever the Unwanted House Guest cleans up before bedtime. Do the same to the bath towels in the morning.

3. *Sheeeeeet!* Short-sheet the beds. An old trick, but it's still really, really funny.

4. *Wet the Appetite:* Install waterbeds in the guest room and then prick them with a little hole right before the Unwanted House Guest falls into a deep slumber.

5. *Food for Thought:* Leave the refrigerator entirely empty except for a month-old lump of raw hamburger meat wrapped up in a ball of tinfoil in the very back of the bottom shelf. A rotting cucumber with mold on the skin would be good for effect as well.

6. *Amish You So Much!* Inform the Unwanted House Guest that you are now Amish and do not use electricity of any sort. Hand the Unwanted House Guest a single candle with some matches.

7. *Sex It Up:* Leave sex toys and contraptions all over the apartment. Dildos, those swing things, lotions and potions, gerbils . . . you get the idea.

⑧ *Heat of the Moment:* Paint all the windows shut, then turn up the heat just enough to cook the Unwanted House Guest medium-rare.

⑨ *Pest-a-Sighed:* Go to the local pet store right before the Unwanted House Guest arrives and purchase a few rodents, maybe a tarantula or two. Let them loose in the guest bedroom.

⑩ *On the Runs:* Feed your dog or cat something that will make it really, really sick with diarrhea all night.

• DAMAGE CONTROL •

PARENT SPEAK

Every Smart Girl knows that parents have a language all their own. They communicate via an ancient coded dialect called Parent Speak. They never mean what they say; and never say what they mean. So, the key to beating your folks at their own game is understanding the subtle nuances of Parent Speak.

Here are handy translations for some of the more common Parent Speak communications.

What Dad Says: "Go ask your mother."
What Dad Means: "I'm too busy building this model of a 1945 Tiger tank to answer you."

What Mom Says: "Please don't make a big deal out of Mother's Day. I really couldn't care less about it."
What Mom Means: "If there aren't a dozen long-stem roses on my doorstep by 6 a.m. I will hunt you down and kill you."

What Dad Says: "Your mother and I have agreed to pay for your wedding."
What Dad Means: "Your guests will be eating off of paper plates, with plastic spoons and forks, and your Uncle Bob's retirement

community band is gonna play for us in exchange for a free bucket of Kentucky Fried Chicken."

What Dad Says: "Feel free to come to me if you ever need to talk."
What Dad Means: "Feel free to come to me if you ever need to talk . . . about anything that doesn't involve sex, drugs, your boyfriends, bra shopping, or anything that will take longer than five minutes to sort out."

What Mom Says: "I support you no matter what you do."
What Mom Means: "I support you as long as I agree with what you are doing."

What Dad Says: "How's work?"
What Dad Means: "Can you hand me the remote?"

What Mom Says: "Your new boyfriend seems very nice."
What Mom Means: "I hate him."

What Dad Says: "This is my daughter . . ."
What Dad Means: "This is *not* my lover."

What Mom Says: "You seem depressed."
What Mom Means: "I'm very depressed and you seem happy, so I'm going to make you miserable."

What Dad Says: "Yes, I'm listening."
What Dad Means: "I haven't been listening to a word you've said since you were two."

What Mom Says: "No, I'm not mad. Really."
What Mom Means: "I'm very, very mad."

> **TOP FIVE THINGS TO NEVER SAY AT A FAMILY FUNERAL**
>
> ① "Well, he was pretty old."
> ② "Where's the food?"
> ③ "I never liked him anyway."
> ④ "He looks better dead than alive!"
> ⑤ "Gee, black really *isn't* that slimming on you, huh?"

What Dad Says: "Your new boyfriend seems like a very nice guy."
What Dad Means: "Well, at least you're not a lesbian."

What Mom Says: "Your apartment is so quaint."
What Mom Means: "You're living like a filthy pig and I hate your place."

• BRINGING OUT YOUR INNER SMART GIRL •

THE SMART GIRL FAMILY COMMANDMENTS

Family is always going to drive you nuts. Some relative will inevitably get on your nerves. You can't change that. But what you *can* change is your response to your family's insanity. These helpful spiritual tips may just keep you sane!

1. *Bite Your Tongue:* Family is different from anything else in your life because it is permanent. You cannot return or exchange for store credit your perfect brother or your bitchy sister or your deadbeat father or your overbearing mother. You are stuck with your family for the rest of your life . . . until either you or they die. So, no matter how much they grate on your nerves, regardless of how hard they push your buttons, bite your tongue. Think before you speak.

2. *Do It Your Way:* When possible, see relatives at your convenience, not theirs. This way you are more likely to be in a good mood and won't resent them.

3. *Multitask:* Incorporate family visits with something you want to do. Forced to traipse halfway across the country for the holidays with your fat sister? Get some skiing in! Have to go to a family reunion in the city? Take this opportunity to do some shopping at the fancy stores, maybe take in a show. You won't resent familial obligations so much when you come home with a really cute purse.

PART FIVE

The General Public

Public Is Just "Pubic" with an "L" in It

● ● ●

Ten Signs You're a Pushover in Public

1. You apologize when someone steps on your foot.

2. You take the seat on the bus with the poop stain on it.

3. You thank the grocery store cashier for placing the gallon of milk on top of the eggs.

4. You don't hang up immediately on telemarketers.

5. You overtip the Chinese food delivery guy for fear of him not liking you.

6. You let street mimes use you as a human prop.

7. You think it's okay that your gynecologist laughs at your body during your exam.

8. You hand-deliver letters across country because you're afraid the teller at the post office will yell at you.

9. You clean up after other people's dogs.

10. You thank the dentist for drilling your teeth without Novocain.

So, you've fought back against rotten relatives, crazy coworkers, bad boyfriends, and frustrating friends. Life should be a breeze for you now. But it isn't. Why? Because no matter how many of your ducks you have in a row at work and in your personal life, you still have to move about the outside world and deal with public nuisances. The motormouths who ruin your movie-going experience at the local theater. The telemarketers who call in the middle of your dinner to sell you magazine subscriptions. The mass transit workers who pull the bus away after you've run thirty blocks to catch it. And don't forget the grocer who packs your heaviest purchase on top of your most fragile one.

Yes, sometimes just leaving the house can be an exercise in self-control. Everywhere you turn there is someone, somewhere, looking to make your life just a little bit harder. Well, it's time to fight back against these public nuisances! Make them wish they had never messed with you! Or live out the rest of your days as a hermit. But that's just creepy.

CHAPTER 37

The Movie Motormouth

(Latin: *Can you hear-us me-us now?*)

● OBSERVED BEHAVIOR IN NATURAL HABITAT ●

This is the butthead who sits directly in front of you, behind you, or right next to you in a perfectly empty movie theater. He then proceeds to talk through the entire film, either on the cell phone he refuses to turn off, to his companion, or worse, to the movie screen! And he inevitably waits until the most pivotal instant in the film, the moment when you can least afford to miss the dialogue, to open his impossibly tightly sealed packages of licorice.

● OFTEN HEARD SAYING ●

"Why is it so quiet in here?"

"LOOK OUT! MICHAEL MYERS IS BEHIND YOU!"

"Hello? Yeah, I'm in a movie right now. Speak up. My cell phone keeps cutting out."

"Why is this movie so loud?"

"Uh, oh, I just dropped my popcorn."

● WHY YOU MUST TAKE ACTION ●

Unfortunately for you, there is one of these buttheads in every theater. With his incessant chattering and complete disregard for the viewing pleasure of others, the Movie Motormouth ruins every theater experience you have. You have a right to actually *hear* the movie you went to see (and eat popcorn that's been sitting at the concession stand since the early '80s). Shut the Movie Motormouth up before he *(gasp!)* forces you to start reading books! You paid for that movie, and you are darn well going to be able to enjoy it! Besides, you have a lot of money riding on the Oscar pool at work this year.

● IT'S REVENGE TIME! ●

Plain and simple. If you can't enjoy the movie, why the heck should this putz be allowed to?

THE SUBTLE APPROACH

The End Is Near: Go to a movie you have already seen and take a seat directly behind the Movie Motormouth. Just as the lights go down and the opening credits begin to roll, whisper to no one in particular, "I can't believe everyone dies at the end of this thing!"

THE NOT-SO-SUBTLE APPROACH

Y'all Come Back Sometime: Wear a ten-gallon cowboy hat to the movie theater and sit directly in front of the Movie Motormouth. If, in an attempt to improve his view of the screen, he moves one seat over, well then, Missy, you move one seat over. If he moves three seats to the right, you and your hat move three seats to the right. See how fun this game of musical movie chairs is? Basically block his view until he stomps off in a huff and goes home. Chances are he will leave behind an un-opened bag of licorice or two. Major bonus!

THE YOU'RE GOING TO HELL APPROACH

Fill 'er Up: Eat a bunch of gassy food on your way to the theater. Then let out a series of room-clearing farts during the movie. It will be impossible for the Movie Motormouth to stay in your general vicinity without endangering his own life. Heck, with the right combination of rice and beans, you'll have the entire *theater* to yourself in no time.

• TOP THREE GIFTS TO GIVE THE MOVIE MOTORMOUTH •

1 A membership to Netflix.

2 A book.

3 A muzzle.

CHAPTER 38

The Insensitive Male Gynecologist

(Latin: *Pokerus and proderus of the ovaries*)

• OBSERVED BEHAVIOR IN NATURAL HABITAT •

Armed with rubber gloves and glorified salad tongs in hand, this is one of the most loathsome creatures in the free world. Without so much as shaking your hand or smiling at you, he pokes and prods at your innards as though you are a science experiment rather than a human being. He never bothers to warn you when something will either feel cold, feel gooey, pinch, or just plain hurt. He squishes your breasts and flicks at your nipples with the sensitivity of a man picking out melons at a fruit stand, and he digs around your ovaries with the same gentle touch he employs to scoop out loose change from under the sofa cushions. And when you ask him a question during the exam (like, "Must you really use those things?") he responds by talking into your vagina rather than to your face. And he doesn't even have the decency to buy you dinner first!

• OFTEN HEARD SAYING •

"Scoot down."

"This giant crowbar I'm inserting might pinch a bit."

"Hmm. I've never seen an ovary do that before."

"Are you practicing safe sex?"

"I really wish you had shaved your legs, Miss."

• WHY YOU MUST TAKE ACTION •

A good doctor is hard to find; and a good vagina doctor is even more rare. Few and far between are the male gynecologists who understand how vulnerable a woman feels dressed in a paper gown, lying flat on her back, spread eagle, with her feet up in stirrups. To this creep, you are nothing more than a pair of ovaries and a uterus—a means by which to pay for one more Wedgwood place setting in his dining room. Now, you may have had your share of female problems and bothered this man countless times with queries about the difference between herpes and a cold sore. But you still deserve to be treated with some respect. Some sensitivity. After all, you're paying for this crap.

• IT'S REVENGE TIME! •

The great thing about exacting vengeance on the Insensitive Male Gynecologist is the host of fun props you can use!

THE SUBTLE APPROACH

Playing Footsie: Just when the good doctor has positioned himself between your legs, let your feet slip out from the heels of the stirrups and right into his face. Do this until all of his front teeth are on the floor.

THE NOT-SO-SUBTLE APPROACH

Put Up a Stink About It: Poking around your nether regions for three minutes per visit is easy money for the Insensitive Male Gynecologist. So, make him really earn that cash. The moment he has wheeled his little chair across the room and positioned himself comfortably in between your legs, let out a stinky fart right in his face. He will have no choice but to continue the examination, despite your noxious fumes. Trust us, that'll be the hardest $300 bucks he's ever had to work for.

THE YOU'RE GOING TO HELL APPROACH

Fried Lice: Lice. Highly contagious and mobile. So you are going to do all you can to get a case of them on your pubes. Rub your genitals up against a homeless guy. Spend the night with a hooker. Whatever you have to do to get those critters running around your private parts. Then, during your exam, "scoot" yourself down real close to the Insensitive Male Gynecologist's head. Your little friends will hop right onto his receding hairline. Then he'll really be bringing his work home with him . . .

• TOP THREE GIFTS TO GIVE THE INSENSITIVE MALE GYNECOLOGIST •

1. Trick rubber gloves with the thumbs missing.

2. An examination room stool with a missing wheel.

3. Your newborn child.

CHAPTER 39

The Sadistic Dentist

(Latin: *Freakus with a drillus*)

• OBSERVED BEHAVIOR IN NATURAL HABITAT •

Some men fantasize about bedding supermodels. This man fantasizes about scraping your gums until they bleed and drilling your molars until they split. If he could, he'd pull out each of your teeth, one by one, without giving you so much as a drop of Novocain. He opens your jaw wider than it is meant to be opened, pokes at your gums, and relishes in the opportunity to shove giant, semi-sterile implements of torture into your mouth under the guise of "cleaning your teeth." He enjoys watching you squirm as that saliva-sucking tube also sucks up your tongue, and seems truly elated when he finds a cavity he can go after. He jams his fingers down your throat, and then asks you a question you cannot possibly answer because, well, his fingers are jammed down your throat. And the jerk doesn't even give you a lollipop afterward.

• OFTEN HEARD SAYING •

"Now, spit."

"Have you been flossing regularly?"

"Your insurance won't cover this."

"Now bite down."

"Yay! You need root canal!"

• WHY YOU MUST TAKE ACTION •

Just because your teeth must be cleaned once a year does *not* entitle this drill-happy jerk-off to treat your mouth like a playground for his deviant inclinations. You use your teeth, tongue, and lips for a lot of things: eating, speaking, that thing you do that's illegal in forty-eight states. So, the last thing you need is an aching mouth after every visit. Your dentist may be a sadist, but you sure as heck aren't a masochist. Bite back at this tooth psycho before you have no teeth left to bite him with. Let the Sadistic Dentist feel your pain . . . literally.

• IT'S REVENGE TIME! •

If you wanted to be in pain, you would spend the day with your family, right?

THE SUBTLE APPROACH

The Spit Take: Make a few choice improvements to the Sadistic Dentist's office when he isn't looking. Slather Vaseline all over the chair so that you keep slipping off it during the exam. Rewire the spit sink so that it squirts him in the eye. Take out the bulb in that ridiculous headlight thing he wears on his head. Oh, and hide all his cotton balls! Anything and everything to make this appointment a little harder on him, and a lot more fun for you.

THE NOT-SO-SUBTLE APPROACH

Lady MacBreath: Nice and simple. Scream the following during your routine teeth cleaning with the Sadistic Dentist. "OH!

THE PAIN IS UNBEARABLE! OH MY GOD, WHY HAVE YOU FORESAKEN ME! KILL ME NOW! HE-E-ELP! THE BLOOD! THE PAIN!" Right before you leave the office douse the front of your blouse with some ketchup. Then stumble into the waiting room and collapse. Chances are the Sadistic Dentist will lose a few patients after that performance. And that, in turn, smacks him right where it hurts—in his wallet.

THE YOU'RE GOING TO HELL APPROACH

Bite Me: Simple. Every time the Sadistic Dentist sticks his fingers in your mouth, bite down as hard as you can. Take a finger tip off for good measure.

● TOP THREE GIFTS TO GIVE THE SADISTIC DENTIST ●

1. A necklace made of all your used dental floss.

2. A copy of *The Marathon Man* on DVD.

3. A box of taffy.

CHAPTER 40

The Corporate Cell Phone Abuser

(Latin: *Blabberus mouthus*)

● OBSERVED BEHAVIOR IN NATURAL HABITAT ●

She barrels down the street, briefcase in hand, jabbering away into the cell phone that is permanently attached to her ear. She dresses in beige designer suits, with beige designer stockings and beige designer pumps, and shouts so loudly into her mobile phone that people on another continent can hear what she's saying. Whether she is discussing business, her babysitter's schedule, her impending divorce, or the genital warts she just contracted, this creature's conversation is the most important thing on the planet. And if she can't find anyone to call on her cell, she still won't put the darn thing away. Instead, she'll wallow away the hours checking her voice mail . . . or texting a message . . . or changing the ring tone . . . checking her voice mail again . . . texting a message, AGAIN! The madness never stops.

● OFTEN HEARD SAYING ●

"BUY! BUY!"

"SELL! SELL!"

"No, this isn't insider trading. Just shut up and listen . . ."

"Have my secretary's secretary call your secretary's secretary."

"What? Hello? I can't hear you. You're breaking up."

• WHY YOU MUST TAKE ACTION •

The advent of the cellular communications system most certainly has its advantages. But using a mobile phone is not a right; it is a privilege. The Corporate Cell Phone Abuser takes advantage of this privilege to no end, and your sanity is suffering because of it. You were not put on this planet to listen to some obnoxious woman, juggling too many gadgets and too few manners, organize her life in your ear. Her penchant for yapping in public spaces is invading your privacy. Give it back to her tenfold.

• IT'S REVENGE TIME! •

There is a law against littering. A law against hunting endangered animals. And a law against wearing Spandex leggings—at least there should be. But until babbling obtrusively in public on a cell phone is deemed illegal by Congress, it's up to you to keep the Corporate Cell Phone Abuser in check.

THE SUBTLE APPROACH

The Shadow Effect: Regardless of whatever brisk pace the Corporate Cell Phone Abuser is traveling at, catch up to her and then keep a steady pace beside her. Pull out your own cell phone (if you don't have one, a makeup compact will suffice) and begin your own, very loud, very fake argument with your mother on your "phone." The louder the Corporate Cell Phone Abuser raises her voice to drown you out, the louder you get. Got it?

THE NOT-SO-SUBTLE APPROACH

The Dead Ringer: The Corporate Cell Phone Abuser lives to talk on her mobile device. So, as she sits beside you on a crowded bus, or at the local library, poised for her next obtrusive call, make fake ringing noises every 3.4 minutes. Each ring will cause her to jump out of her seat, snap open her cell, and scream, "HELLO! HELLO! IS ANYONE THERE?"

THE YOU'RE GOING TO HELL APPROACH

The Breakup: As the Corporate Cell Phone Abuser is jabbering away, reach over with your hand and snap off the antenna on her cell. Then toss it in the nearest sewer. Her call will be dropped instantly.

● TOP THREE GIFTS TO GIVE THE CORPORATE CELL PHONE ABUSER ●

1 A cell phone that doesn't open.

2 A cell phone that doesn't ring.

3 A cell phone that isn't a cell phone at all: it's a Pez dispenser.

CHAPTER 41

The Line Jumper

(Latin: *Cutterus of the queues*)

● OBSERVED BEHAVIOR IN NATURAL HABITAT ●

Be it at the bank, the post office, the department of motor vehicles, or the local movie theater, this person pops around from point to point, slinking her way up to the head of the line from the very back of the line. She will do anything and everything to get ahead of the people who stand between her and the teller. From faking a heart attack to pulling the fire alarm, this creature is determined to beat everyone to the pot of gold. Her eyes are constantly roving around in search of an elderly person she can cut or a blind person she can shove backward. She has never waited for a thing in her life.

● OFTEN HEARD SAYING ●

"No, I was here before you. You just didn't see me."

"I think I'm having a heart attack. I need to get in front of the line."

"Ooops. I didn't see you there."

"I'm blind. I didn't realize I was cutting you."

"Oh, I was here. I just stepped off to get something."

● WHY YOU MUST TAKE ACTION ●

When you arrive at, say, the post office or the bank and there is a huge line, you simply get on the back and wait like everyone else, right? You don't do this because you have nothing better to do but wait; you do this because that is the point of a line—to provide first-come, first-served service to people in need of customer care. But the Line Jumper? She thinks that she has the right to roll out of bed ten minutes before the post office closes and cut to the front of the line. And every time she cuts you, she knocks you one person further back in the line. And that means you have fewer minutes left in your life to spend doing the important things—like watching TV.

● IT'S REVENGE TIME! ●

Some of the sneakiest, most manipulative and downright rude people can be found jumping the lines of your life. Show them that you are keeping your place no matter what.

THE SUBTLE APPROACH

Line Dancing: Rearrange the line ropes and start a fake line. The Line Jumper will follow you, and so will some other brainless idiots. Eventually everyone from the real line will move end up standing on the fake one, thinking they've discovered a loophole. Then, just as the teller dings the "Next!" light, run back to where the real line was and sachet up to the window. You'll be out of there in no time.

THE NOT-SO-SUBTLE APPROACH

Heel Thyself: The next time the Line Jumper sneaks her way in front of you, repeatedly kick the back of her heels with the toe of your shoe. Eventually, you will kick hard enough to knock her on her boney ass. Then just step over her and get back into the place that was rightfully yours.

THE YOU'RE GOING TO HELL APPROACH

Put Up Yer Pukes: Whenever the Line Jumper cuts in front of you, jab your finger down your throat until your gag reflexes kick in. Then vomit on her back. The more chunky and frothy, the better. She will be forced to get off line to go rinse off . . . and so will a bunch of the people ahead of her who can't stand the stink. That's when you mosey on up to the front of the line for a breath of fresh air!

• TOP THREE GIFTS TO GIVE THE LINE JUMPER •

1 A sign that reads "Line Forms Here."

2 Shoes with glue on the soles.

3 An electric dog collar that zaps her every time she moves.

CHAPTER 42

The Relentless Telemarketer

(Latin: *Dinnerus interruptus*)

• OBSERVED BEHAVIOR IN NATURAL HABITAT •

Using mysterious telepathic talents, this creature can sense the precise moment you sit down to eat your dinner at home. It is at this very moment that she will dial your phone number and attempt to sell you swamp land in Arkansas. She doesn't care if you are in the middle of dinner or labor—she will keep you on the phone until your fish sticks are cold as ice. Relentless in her goal to sell you stuff you don't need, and intellectually incapable of understanding the word "no," she will sooner call you back every hour, on the hour, than take your name off her call list as you request. She *will* sell you that Arkansas swamp land if it's the last thing she does!

• OFTEN HEARD SAYING •

"This won't take long."

"I just need a moment of your time."

"Am I speaking with the head of the household?"

"No, Ma'am, this isn't a scam."

"I'll call back."

● WHY YOU MUST TAKE ACTION ●

How many more delicious dinners are you going to have ruined because you made the mistake of answering your phone? What is the point of having locks on your doors if some stranger in Oregon can harass you to no end via the phone? You have been way too nice to this troublemaker in the past. It is time to take back your privacy. (Besides, you can't afford that swamp land in Arkansas.)

● IT'S REVENGE TIME! ●

The Relentless Telemarketer has made a career out of harassing you on the phone. Show her what being trapped on the phone is really like!

THE SUBTLE APPROACH

The Repeat Offender: The Relentless Telemarketer lives off of her commissions. That means she must make as many calls as is humanly possible each night. So, you are going to do whatever it takes to keep this phone harasser on the line with you, and waste her precious time. Pretend you don't hear too well and make her repeat everything she says. Twice. Eventually, she'll just hang up on you. And that means you can go back to your fish sticks!

THE NOT-SO-SUBTLE APPROACH

So Glad You Called: If the Relentless Telemarketer feels she knows you well enough to bother you at home, then she is certainly a close enough friend for you to discuss all your personal problems with, right? The moment she finishes saying, "Hi, I'm calling with an extraordinary offer for you . . ." break into a lengthy monologue about how glad you are to hear from her, and how much you are looking forward to this new friendship. You know, since you had that really unhappy childhood and all.

What with all the abuse and neglect . . . not to mention your tendency to date the wrong guys. "I'll start at the beginning. Let's see, first I was born . . ."

THE YOU'RE GOING TO HELL APPROACH

Screaming Your Calls: Whenever you answer your ringing phone and it is the Relentless Telemarketer on the other end, simply scream into the phone. Do this enough times and eventually she'll lose her hearing.

• TOP THREE GIFTS TO GIVE THE RELENTLESS TELEMARKETER •

1. A wet phone book.

2. A jaw breaker candy.

3. A rotary phone.

CHAPTER 43

The Angry Bus Driver

(Latin: *Dictatorus at the wheelus*)

● OBSERVED BEHAVIOR IN NATURAL HABITAT ●

This creature is usually severely overweight and boasts an attitude the size of Wisconsin. And despite the fact that he barely passed his driver's test, this creature holds your future in the palm of his steering hands. He refuses to smile or acknowledge your cheerful greetings in the morning, and glares at you if you dare to ask a question about the bus route. He watches in the rearview mirror for the precise moment you let go of the hand rail to lurch the bus to a sudden stop. If he didn't get laid the night before, he's going to make you stand out in the pouring rain while he sits in the dry bus on break. And if you don't have exact change? Well, God help you.

● OFTEN HEARD SAYING ●

"Exact change!"

"This bus doesn't stop there."

"I dunno."

"I said, I dunno."

"Get off my bus!"

• WHY YOU MUST TAKE ACTION •

When you think about it, it is really quite silly for you live in fear of a man who drives a giant tube for a living. What are you so scared of? You are a paying customer and deserve to be treated with respect. Besides, you need this bus. It's not like you can walk to work in those ridiculous shoes you're wearing, dear.

• IT'S REVENGE TIME! •

You have been jostled, jerked, and yelled at one too many times by this steering wheel–happy freak. Fight back . . . and maybe even get a free ride out of it!

THE SUBTLE APPROACH

Roll with It: Rent a wheelchair for the day. This means the Angry Bus Driver will have to drag his lard ass out of the chair and walk all the way to the back of the bus to activate the hand-icapped lift. Keep rolling off the ramp while he's operating the elevator feature. This will hold up his entire schedule and get him in trouble with the boss. And the wrongful injury lawsuit you'll be filing a few months from now will really piss him off!

THE NOT-SO-SUBTLE APPROACH

Oh, Canada! Drop Canadian coins into the change box. This will hold up the entire bus because the Angry Bus Driver will either have to watch you try and fish out the coins, or actually help you. Either way, it will ruin his day. And if you stuff just enough Canadian coins in there, they will get stuck. And that means the whole bus gets to ride for free. You'll be a hero to the rest of the passengers.

THE YOU'RE GOING TO HELL APPROACH

Meat Your Maker: Think about it. The Angry Bus Driver spends eight to ten hours on that bus. Ventilation is poor. So, leaving a hunk of month-old roast beef tucked in between the two back-seats will give him something to really remember you by. It will be days before the Angry Bus Driver discovers the source of the stink. And by then, he will probably have contracted some sort of *E. Coli*–based disease from your little present.

● TOP THREE GIFTS TO GIVE THE ANGRY BUS DRIVER ●

❶   Your middle finger.

❷   Your middle finger with glitter on it.

❸   Your middle finger with a booger on it.

CHAPTER 44

The Talentless Street Mime

(Latin: *Stuckus in a boxus*)

● OBSERVED BEHAVIOR IN NATURAL HABITAT ●

Try as you might to slip unnoticed by this nitwit with the painted white face and black polyester pants so tight you can see his testicles, he spots you in the crowd of fans who have gathered around his park bench. He points to you and pantomimes his heart beating out of his shirt. You lower your head and walk faster. He gestures to the audience, points to you again, raises an eyebrow, and the crowd cheers in encouragement. Then he tosses out his invisible rope and begins pulling himself toward you. The crowd cheers louder as you scream "No! Get away from me! You don't have a real rope!" But before you know it, the Talentless Street Mime has pulled you center stage into his little "circle of entertainment." And for the next ten minutes he makes you pretend you are stuck in a box, pulls imaginary ribbons out of your ears, and rubs his pelvic area just a little too close to your butt for comfort as he pretends you two are walking against invisible wind. The crowd laughs and tosses dollar bills into the top hat he has placed in the center of the circle. And if you dare not put some money in that smelly hat, too? Well, you have an angry mob scene on your hands.

● OFTEN HEARD SAYING ●

(Nothing, jackass. He's a mime!)

• WHY YOU MUST TAKE ACTION •

Think about it for a moment. Why do you drag your boney butt out of bed each morning? Because you have a job, right? And why do you have that job? Because you need to make money. And how do you make that money? You *earn* it! By *working*! So, does it make sense that you should hand over your hard-earned money to this talentless, tongue-less twit who does nothing but humiliate people in public with his imaginary props?? He doesn't even pay taxes on that 'seventy-five cents a day he collects!

• IT'S REVENGE TIME! •

Street performers depend on the kindness of strangers. Well, the Talentless Street Mime is going to find out that not every stranger is so kind.

THE SUBTLE APPROACH

Can You Spare Some Change? Every time the Talentless Street Mime shoves that stupid hat in your face, looking for some cash, smile excitedly and say, "Why thank you, sir!" Then reach into said hat and grab a few quarters. These will come in handy when you need to do laundry.

THE NOT-SO-SUBTLE APPROACH

Seeing Double: Toss on a black leotard and tights, paint your face white, and set up shop two feet away from the Talentless Street Mime. Do a few "oh, I'm stuck in a box and will now try to get out" gestures, maybe pretend to walk against heavy wind once or twice. Only incorporate two assets the Talentless Street Mime is not so lucky to have: your boobies. A little cleavage here and there for the passers-by might just mean filet mignon for dinner for you.

THE YOU'RE GOING TO HELL APPROACH

Nuts About You: The next time the Talentless Street Mime makes you an unwilling participant in one of his stupid pantomimes, kick him in the nuts with your knee. Knocking the wind out of a guy's testicles has a magical way of making even the most silent of mimes scream at the top of his lungs. And a screaming mime ain't no mime at all. There go those tips.

• TOP THREE GIFTS TO GIVE THE TALENTLESS STREET MIME •

1. A real rope.

2. A real box.

3. Monopoly money.

CHAPTER 45

The Grumpy Grocery Store Cashier

(Latin: *Smasherus of the eggsus*)

● OBSERVED BEHAVIOR IN NATURAL HABITAT ●

She thinks nothing of dropping the gallon of milk right on top of the egg carton, or tossing the fresh-baked pie you just bought upside down in the grocery bag. She grumbles if you ask for a price check and then rolls her eyes if you dare to put that item back because it costs too much. She refuses to move the conveyor belt up when you stand there on the line with your arms filled with groceries. But the minute you begin placing the items on the conveyor belt in an orderly fashion she makes the conveyor belt move about 60 mph so everything goes flying onto the floor. And good luck if you try to cash in a coupon!

● OFTEN HEARD SAYING ●

"Paper or plastic?"

"We're not accepting that coupon."

"PRICE CHECK FOR THE VAGINAL ITCH LOTION ON AISLE 5!"

"Ten items or less, lady! Read the sign!"

"I'm closed."

• WHY YOU MUST TAKE ACTION •

Food. It is the staple of life. Without it, you will die. (Of course, then you'll finally fit into that bikini you bought while under the influence on Spring Break . . . but we digress.) However, inconvenient though it may be, food does not just magically arrive in your cupboards. So, at some point you are going to have to deal with the Grumpy Grocery Store Cashier. Don't live in fear of this woman. And don't take a chance of missing out on the toilet paper sale!

• IT'S REVENGE TIME! •

The only thing that stands in between you and your next meal is this nasty little nincompoop. She thought she had reason to be pissy this morning? She ain't seen nothing yet.

THE SUBTLE APPROACH

Divide and Conquer: You know that separator thing you're supposed to put in between your groceries and those of the person behind you on the conveyor belt? Well. Toss it in your purse when no one is looking. Then make sure to keep sliding your groceries against the conveyor belt's current until all your stuff is mixed in with the stuff of the guy behind you. When the Grumpy Grocery Store Cashier accidentally charges you for his peanut butter, freak out and call the police.

THE NOT-SO-SUBTLE APPROACH

Just One More Thing: Just as the Grumpy Grocery Store Cashier rings up your total, announce that you forgot to pick one important item up and leave the line. She cannot do anything because your grocery bill is tying up the register. She has no choice but to wait. Meanwhile, you just take your time sauntering over to the other end of the grocery store.

THE YOU'RE GOING TO HELL APPROACH

Cha-ching! Pay for your grocery order in pennies.

• TOP THREE GIFTS TO GIVE THE GRUMPY GROCERY STORE CASHIER •

1 Your broken eggs.

2 A personal check (without ID).

3 Wet coupons.

CHAPTER 46

Smart Girl Tricks of the Trade

How to Get Even by Getting Over

Unless you want to spend the rest of your life holed up in your home, avoiding human contact of any kind, you must learn how to mingle with the masses. It isn't as hard as you think.

• HOW TO STAND OUT IN A CROWD •

Crowds. You have to deal with them in public on a regular basis. Crowded buses, crowded grocery stores, crowded shopping malls. They are all around at any given time. And with so many people squished together in tight spaces—each of them believing that they should be the first priority—it is easy to get, well, lost in the crowd.

But the Smart Girl knows there are some very special ways to make yourself the center of attention. Ways in which you can make your presence known, and get what you want before everyone else. Here are just a few.

1. Stuck waiting on a really long line to buy tickets to the latest summer blockbuster movie? Try not bathing for a solid week. No one likes to stand in front of, next to, or behind a stinky person with greasy hair and unshaved armpits. You'll be the first one in the theater—and better yet, get the whole front row to yourself.

2   Wear an outfit made entirely out of barbed wire. A barbed-wire dress, coat, hat, shoes. Trust us, you'll be given your space.

3   Nothing intimidates commuters on a crowded train more than a bleeder. So, the next time you really want to get a seat, arrive onto the train with ketchup doused all over your face and shirt. Nobody will bother to call 9–1–1 for you, of course, lest it keep them from reading the morning paper. But they will most certainly give you some much-wanted space. (After all, who wants blood all over their business suit, right?)

• DAMAGE CONTROL •

DEALING WITH A CASHIER WHO
REFUSES TO BEND THE RULES

Stuck with a cashier who won't refund your money? Or is charging you full price on an item you earnestly believe should be on sale? These suckers for protocol can be your worst enemy. Or are they? Try employing some of the following suggestions to turn the tide in your favor.

1   *Return the Favor:* Say you bought a dress a while back. And you wore it a few times, but now realize you look like crap in it (thanks to your friend telling you, "Hey, you look like crap in that dress."). You want to return it, but you don't have the receipt. No problem. Simply shoot a few staples into the hem of the dress, take it back to the store, and put a really indignant look on your face. When you reach the counter, slam your fist down, pull out the dress, and announce that you were recently the guest of honor at a very highbrow fund-raiser for mentally handicapped children, and wore this dress for the first time, only to discover that "one of your employees clearly thought it was funny to put a damaged item of clothing on the rack and sell it." The cashier will be so afraid of a lawsuit that she'll instantly issue you a full refund. And that's money you can use to buy a dress you don't look like crap in.

② *The Really Free Gift:* Most cosmetic companies at your local mall give away really cool free gifts. Only trouble is, these "free" gifts are not really free at all, because you have to purchase, like, $500 bucks' worth of face cream to get them. This is how we rationalize this next, slightly crooked, revenge tactic. If you see a "free with the purchase of . . ." gift you really want, buy whatever mandatory amount of goods you have to in order to qualify for the "free" gift. Then bring the unopened purchased items back, along with the receipt, about a week later. Explain that you have changed your mind about the products. When the cashier declares that you must also return the "free" gift, gasp in horror and exclaim, "What free gift? I never got one!"

③ *Dining Out:* So you tried to slip your expired coupons past the grocery store clerk but she caught you. Don't worry—the food court in the mall is an ideal way to cut your grocery bill in half. From free samples of crackers and hot dog bites to yogurt smoothie shots and chocolate treats, the food court serves up pretty much everything your tummy desires. All for free. So, make a point of visiting the mall every single morning on your way to work. Grab as many free samples from every single food court stand you can get your grubby little hands on. Fill up, then go to work. Repeat on the way home for dinner, and you can keep yourself pretty much fed for nothing! Just bring some antacid . . .

• THE SMART GIRL PUBLIC COMMANDMENTS •

① *Kill 'em with Kindess:* Some mean people are mean because they just expect people not to like them. So, why not try some reverse psychology? Spread some sunshine in an angry person's life. Surprise the Angry Bus Driver with some fresh-baked cookies! Toss a dollar in the Talentless Street Mime's hat. Admire the Grumpy Grocery Store Cashier's hairdo. You may just strike up a friendship with one of these miserable people. And they may turn out to not be so miserable after all!

② *Look Good, Feel Good:* Always look your best when moving about in public. This sounds shallow, but studies show . . . well, okay, there haven't actually been any scientific studies on this matter, but there should be . . . that there is a direct correlation between looks and confidence. In other words, if you are feeling attractive, you will exude confidence. And people, even really mean people, will be just a little more intimidated by you. And that means you hold the power.

③ *End of Days:* Never ever schedule your gynecology or dental appointments for the morning before you go to work. You will end up carrying your hatred for them over into the rest of your day. Instead, always schedule your appointments for after work—this way you can rest your weary soul at home after being violated, taking comfort in a soft couch and myriad hours of bad television. (Not to mention the fact you get out of work early!)

● TOP FIVE THINGS NEVER TO SAY TO YOUR WAITER ●

"I need to send this back."

"Do you have your green card?"

"Can you repeat the Specials of the Day?"

"I don't have cash on me."

"I only tip 5 percent, no matter how good the service is."

The "What Have You Learned?" Quiz

So, here we are at the end. You've successfully fought back against bad coworkers, annoying relatives, selfish friends, and dangerous exes. You've learned how to stand up for yourself, take no crap, and generally have a new lease on life. If you were paying attention, you should now head out into the world a revived, confident Smart Girl just full of surprises.

Take this simple test to see how far you've come.

● HOW TO TAKE THIS TEST ●

Find a quiet place in your house . . . or the refrigerator box you've been sleeping in under the bridge. Take out a # 2 pencil. (If you do not have a # 2 pencil, steal one from someone who does. If you don't know someone who owns a # 2 pencil, then take a # 1 pencil and a wood-whittling tool—and turn that # 1 into a # 2. Or bid for a # 2 on e-Bay. Just do something so we can move on!) Circle the answer that most applies to your thought process. Then check to see if your answer matches the correct one.

And, listen carefully. There is no reason to go hopping around from middle to back to front of this test. Follow the order in which the questions are given. After all, there is a reason this book was put together in said order and you should respect said order. Don't see *you* with a published book. So keep your trap shut and just follow the instructions, will you! Picking a fight about so petty an issue will only result in you being sued or jailed . . .

• THE QUIZ •

1 Your best friend has recently moved to the other side of the country and has neglected your friendship since. She has not returned your calls, written you her usual daily e-mails, and, even forgot your birthday! The most important day of the year! You:

> a. Hire a hit man to take her out and hide the body parts.
>
> b. Tear up every picture you have of her in your home, toss out any gifts she ever gave you, and stab a voodoo doll in her likeness with a butcher knife repeatedly in the heart.
>
> c. Keep calling her until she finally answers the phone. Then ask her if everything is okay between the two of you. Ask if there is something you may have unwittingly done to offend her and suggest that you two meet for a girls' weekend to patch things up.
>
> d. Send her an e-mail outlining all the exciting things you are doing with all of your other best friends and mention that it "really doesn't seem like you've even left."

Answer "a" is wrong because it will land you in prison.

Answer "b" is wrong because some of the gifts she gave you are cool.

Answer "c" is wrong because you'll look like a needy schmuck.

The correct answer is "d". Smart Girls know that the best way to get even with someone who has hurt your feelings is to hurt their feelings right back. Revenge is everything.

2 You have been spending way beyond your means lately and suddenly find yourself unable to pay the rent. Your landlord has pasted an eviction notice onto your door ordering you out in thirty days. You:

a. Go out and get a second job to earn that late rent. You got yourself into this mess and must now get yourself out.

b. Trash the place and move in with your parents.

c. Pretend you never noticed the eviction notice and continue living there until you are cuffed by the police and dragged away.

d. Offer to pay your rent in sexual favors.

Answer "a" is wrong because you are too pretty to have to work a second job.

Answer "c" is wrong because you won't look good in prison garb.

And if you don't know why answer "d" is wrong, well, you ought to be ashamed of yourself!

The correct answer is "b": Spraying blood all over the walls and unhooking the plumbing will make it impossible for your landlord to rent the place out, and thereby, he will end up losing more money.

❸ Your mother has come to stay with you for a week. She spends the visit criticizing everything you do wrong in your life: from the way you have decorated your home, to your cooking, your taste in friends and your job. Not to mention she uses up all your expensive shampoo rather than the dishwashing detergent you slipped into an old Pantene bottle. You:

a. Invite her back for Thanksgiving—but in the meantime, move.

b. Change the locks on your doors, so she can't get back in after her run to the grocery store.

c. Short-sheet her bed.

d. Invite your sister over to join the fun.

Answer "b" is wrong because then she'll just camp out on your porch and your neighbors will think you're cruel.

Answer "c" takes too much time—you can barely make a bed correctly.

Answer "d" is just plain stupid—why add to your problems?

The correct answer is "a": You still end up smelling like roses and get a mother-free Thanksgiving next year to boot! You can always claim that you gave her your new address.

4 You and your boyfriend are spending a weekend camping in the mountains when a large Grizzly bear attacks your tent. (One of you imbeciles left a half-eaten Snickers bar in your sleeping bag.) The bear is clearly determined to swallow one of you whole. You:

    a. Stand really still and pretend you are a tree.

    b. Redirect the angry bear to the campers across the way who stole your cooler.

    c. Toss yourself in between your boyfriend and the bear and scream, "Take me, you bastard! Take me!"

    d. Toss your boyfriend in between you and the bear and scream, "Take him, you bastard! Take him!"

Answer "a" is stupid because clearly, you are not a tree.

Answer "c" is wrong because your boyfriend will never appreciate what you did for him, let alone send you a thank-you card.

Answer "d" is wrong because you don't know how to drive a manual car and need him to get you home.

The correct answer is "b": The campers across the way deserve to get eaten. That cooler was expensive.

⑤   Your boss just fired you. He claims that, despite the fact you never missed a day of work and clients rave about your performance, he needs to downsize. He gives you one hour to clean out your desk and leave the premises before he calls security. You:

> a. Toss yourself down the stairs, break both your legs and contact a personal injury lawyer immediately. (Mention that you tripped because you were so upset when your boss tried to grabbed your breasts.)
>
> b. Get down on your knees and offer to do "whatever it takes" to keep your job.
>
> c. Reach for the nearest pencil on his desk and ram it through his jugular.
>
> d. Steal every office supply you can fit in your purse—pencils, pens, notepads, tape, the water cooler. Then leave.

Answer "b" is wrong for the same reason that "2.d" was wrong.

Answer "c" will ruin your blouse.

Answer "d" doesn't work because now that you're unemployed, what use do you have for office supplies really?

The correct answer is "a": The best way to exact revenge on your rotten boss is to defeat the purpose of his money-saving scheme in firing you. A hefty sexual harassment/personal injury lawsuit will tie him up in court for years. And break the company's bank.

⑥   After picking up your suit from the dry cleaners, you return home and try it on only to discover it has shrunk by two sizes. When you take it back to the cleaners the woman behind the register refuses to refund your money, claiming that you clearly got fat in the last three days. You:

> a. Beat the lady over the head with the hanger

and take the money she owes you out of the register.

b. Apologize and put yourself on a strict diet.

c. Trade it for another suit in the shop that looks about your size.

d. Donate the suit to the local charity for Little People and leave the premises. But not before taping a sign on the front door that reads "Closed for Renovations Until Further Notice."

Answer "a" is wrong because hangers don't do enough damage.

Answer "b" won't work because you know you can't maintain a diet.

Answer "c" sucks because the rest of the suits in the joint are made of polyester.

The correct answer is "d": Any woman who steals your money and ruins your designer suit needs to be taught a lesson. The customer is always right—and the customer will go elsewhere when your shop is closed!

• THE WRAP-UP •

Now how did you do on the test?

If you answered 0–2 questions correctly: Well, the bad news is that you are an embarrassment to your gender. The good news is, there is hope. And that hope comes in the form of you going to the bookstore and buying multiple copies of this book. Then plant a copy in your car, your purse, your gym locker, on your nightstand, in your refrigerator, your tampon box—pretty much anywhere and everywhere your little bug eyes are likely to focus at any given time. Study this book until you have mastered every single Smart Girl trick in the book. You *do* have the power to unearth that inner Smart Girl buried deep inside you. Really, you do! She's just dying to get out. (Seriously, she's like suffocating.) Get crackin'!

If you answered 3–5 questions correctly: You are far from a complete failure, but not quite a bona fide Smart Girl yet. So call in sick to work, take the phone off the hook, and tell Mr. Boyfriend and all those annoying gal pals of yours to leave you alone for a few days, because you've got some serious studying to do. Take a hot bath, crawl into bed, and go back to the beginning of this book. Read the whole thing again. Slowly. And this time PAY ATTENTION! Your life depends on it, woman!

If you answered all 6 questions correctly: Congratulations! You are officially a Smart Girl! Ready to take on the world! It is now safe for you to walk among other humans because you will maintain your dignity, and most importantly, control, no matter what happens. So, skip off to that miserable job of yours! Invite your annoying friends over for dinner! Cuddle up with your less-than-perfect boyfriend. Heck, give your mother a call! There is nothing you can't handle now! Oh, and while you're at it, go out and buy like, two hundred copies of this book for all your Not So Smart Girlfriends. Think of all the lives you can save. And who knows? The author might just send you a thank-you card for all the book sales! (Probably not, though—she's pretty stingy with postage stamps.)

Now, go off and be Smart!

There's Always a Bright Side

Learning how to see the bright side of even the most abysmal turn of events is one of the most valuable revenge skills the Smart Girl can master. For nothing will annoy your opponents more than to see you completely un-phased by whatever twists and turns of misery Fate may throw at you. So, bring on the health scares! The car accidents! The financial investment disasters!

Because getting knocked unconscious by a broken lamp post may mean slipping into a coma; but a coma means you don't have to attend Sunday dinner with your family.

● THE BAD NEWS IS . . . ●

The Bad News Is: You caught your boyfriend cheating on you with the cleaning lady.
The Good News Is: She already washed the windows.

The Bad News Is: You just had a huge fight with your mother.
The Good News Is: She does the silent treatment thing for at least two days.

The Bad News Is: You got run over by a car.
The Good News Is: You've been looking a bit fat lately.

The Bad News Is: You didn't get the job promotion.
The Good News Is: It would have meant doing real work.

The Bad News Is: Your marriage just ended.
The Good News Is: So did your very sexy neighbor's.

The Bad News Is: A Great White shark bit your leg off.
The Good News Is: Handicapped parking.

The Bad News Is: You're going blind.
The Good News Is: Blind people get discounts at the movie theater.

The Bad News Is: Brad Pitt took out a restraining order against you.
The Good News Is: George Clooney hasn't yet.

The Bad News Is: You accidentally deleted all your computer files at work.
The Good News Is: Now you have more space to store naked pictures of yourself on the hard drive.

The Bad News Is: Aliens have abducted you.
The Good News Is: There's a food court on board the spaceship.

The Bad News Is: Your rent just doubled.
The Good News Is: So did your ability to forge checks.

The Bad News Is: You have a stalker.
The Good News Is: He's getting very bored.

The Bad News Is: Doctors found a lump in your breast.
The Good News Is: It's your nipple.

The Bad News Is: You only have a few months to live.
The Good News Is: Dead people don't have to pay overdue library fines.

The Bad News Is: Your mother-in-law is coming to live with you.
The Good News Is: She is terminally ill.

The Bad News Is: You have to attend a funeral.
The Good News Is: You look good in black.

The Bad News Is: There's been a death in the family.
The Good News Is: It wasn't yours.

The Bad News Is: There is an office rumor going around that you are gay.
The Good News Is: The more gay Anne Heche was, the more money she made.

The Bad News Is: Your office computer just crashed.
The Good News Is: It's pretty hard to do work without a computer.

The Bad News Is: You have PMS.
The Good News Is: That's free license to lash out at friends and family.

The Bad News Is: Your fiancé just left you at the altar.
The Good News Is: He also left his wallet.

The Bad News Is: Your mother has to be placed in a nursing home.
The Good News Is: Your mother has to be placed in a nursing home.

The Bad News Is: Your wallet was stolen.
The Good News Is: There was nothing of worth in there.

The Bad News Is: You got a really bad haircut.
The Good News Is: There is good money to be made posing for those "What Not to Do" magazine pieces.

The Bad News Is: Drug dealers have invaded your neighborhood.
The Good News Is: They sell Tylenol gel tabs at a great discount.

The Bad News Is: You defaulted on your home loan.
The Good News Is: The annual pig roast at the "Golden Years" Trailer Park.

The Bad News Is: You put on some pounds.
The Good News Is: It's easier to get a seat on the bus when you look pregnant.

The Bad News Is: You have a blind date.
The Good News Is: You aren't looking that great lately anyway.

The Bad News Is: You have love handles.
The Good News Is: They make you easier to hoist.

The Bad News Is: You have a mustache.
The Good News Is: Men get treated with more respect in the workplace.

The Bad News Is: No one came to your birthday party.
The Good News Is: All the more cake for you.

The Bad News Is: There is a serial killer on the loose.
The Good News Is: You've been looking to meet new and exciting people.

The Bad News Is: Your boss gave you a ham rather than a holiday bonus this year.
The Good News Is: Ham gives you that "Can't Go to Work Because My Diarrhea Is So Bad" kinda reaction.

The Bad News Is: The waiter got your order wrong.
The Good News Is: You can get his tip wrong.

The Smart Girl's Greeting Card Collection

When was the last time you went to buy a greeting card for someone and found a card that said what you really wanted to say?

Exactly.

Well, every Smart Girl travels equipped with a stash of greeting cards for those less-traditional occasions Hallmark tends to overlook. So, express yourself. And express yourself loud and clear!

Dear Husband,
sorry I cheated on you . . . but that guy doesn't have erectile dysfunction.

Happy Birthday, Grandma!
Don't forget to put me in your Will.

Sorry I ran over your dog.
He didn't feel a thing . . . except the tire of
my SUV crushing his ribcage into oblivion.

Thanks for another year without a raise, Boss! . . . You suck monkey butt!

To my mother-in-law on her birthday. . . . Screw you and the broomstick you flew in on.

To my darling husband on our anniversary.
I'm so happy we found each other. . . .
By the way . . . Junior isn't yours.

Sorry you've been wrongfully imprisoned
for a crime you did not commit. . . .
Don't drop the soap!

To my mother on Mother's Day. . . .
Please tell me I'm adopted!

Sorry to hear you have Alzheimer's. . . .
Sorry to hear you have Alzheimer's.

Wishing you the best on your Execution day . . . hope this gets to you in time.

Sorry you have cancer . . . but hey, that hairdo wasn't working for you anyway.

Happy Father's Day. . . .
Mommy says you're not my real dad.

Please don't commit suicide . . . before
you return that book I loaned you.

Happy Birthday to the Office Pet . . .
I wouldn't walk home alone in the dark
if I were you tonight.

Sorry we buried your husband alive. . . .
We've credited your account accordingly.

Happy Hanukkah from us Christians . . .
no way we're sending seven more
cards like this.

To the bride on her wedding day . . .
I'm sure he won't cheat on you . . . again.

Thanks for the wedding gift. . . .
Any chance you still have the receipt?

Happy Grandparents' Day. . . .
Please stop knitting me pot holders.

Happy Valentine's Day to my single friend. . . . I'm spending the weekend in Vermont with my wonderful, handsome, and rich husband. Have fun watching TV with the cat!

Congratulations on the birth of your son . . . let's hope he looks like your wife.

Congratulations on your college graduation . . . see you at the drive-thru window!

I hear you're coming out of the closet. . . . What took you so long?

Happy Birthday to my best friend . . .
I'd stay away from that cake, if I were you.
No seriously, you're getting fat.

Tough break—you losing your legs
and all. . . . Guess running the marathon
with me is out of the question now, huh?

Good luck with your new job. . . . Must be nice to have one. I wouldn't know.

So you got fired, eh? No worries. You weren't good at that job anyway.

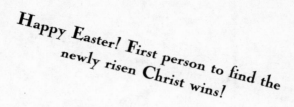

Happy Easter! First person to find the newly risen Christ wins!

Thinking of you. . . . Licking tapioca pudding off my genitals.

Your new hairstyle is great . . . for laughs.

Sisters have a special bond . . . that can only be broken if you do something really bitchy to me.

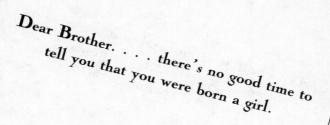

Dear Brother. . . . there's no good time to tell you that you were born a girl.

Congratulations on your gay wedding! Too bad it means nothing in the eyes of the law.

Sorry to hear your husband beat the crap out of you. . . . But let's be honest, you had it coming, right?

APPENDIX D

The Smart Girl's Words to Live By

1   Tomorrow is another day . . . unless you forgot to get a 2007 calendar, in which case tomorrow doesn't really exist for you, now does it?

2   A body in motion remains in motion . . . a body at rest gets really fat.

3   Life is short . . . but midgets are shorter.

4   Every time a bell rings, an angel gets its wings . . . or someone is at the door.

5   All men are created equal . . . equally annoying, that is.

6   'Tis better to receive than to give.

7   Two's company; three's a crowd . . . and one heck of a fun ménage à trois!

8   You are only as good as the last person who talks about you says you are.

9   Don't do today what you can make someone else do for you to-morrow.

10   If you really want something in life, steal it.

11   Money doesn't grow on trees, but paper does . . . and since money is made from paper, technically, you should be able to pay your bills with shrubbery.

12   The friend of your friend's enemy . . . is probably never gonna cross paths with you, so don't worry about it.

13   When life hands you lemons . . . take them back to the store and exchange them for a Twinkie.

14   Keep your friends close and your enemies . . . off your New Year's Eve party mailing list.

15   If something seems too good to be true, it probably is . . . except for chocolate chip cookie dough ice cream. That really does exist.

16   Two wrongs don't make a right . . . they make a left.

17   Beauty is skin deep . . . so get facials.

18   The sky's the limit . . . and your credit card company should understand that.

19   There's no "I" in "team" . . . unless you spell it "TIEAM."

20   No bad deed goes unpunished . . . except in really liberal states.

21   The eyes are the windows to the soul . . . so wear sunglasses at all times.

22   The grass is always greener on the other side . . . unless you live in New York City where there is no grass . . . unless you mean "grass" as in marijuana . . . in which case there's plenty.

23   Follow your bliss . . . unless it's going in the wrong direction.

24   Love is blind . . . and so is Stevie Wonder.

25   Hear no evil, see no evil, do no evil . . . unless you won't get caught.

26   If at first you don't succeed, give up and save yourself the embarrassment.

27   To err is human; to forgive is just stupid.

28   All's fair in love and war . . . except the unfair stuff.

29   'Tis better to have loved and lost than to have loved, gotten sick of the dude, but be stuck with him for eternity.

30   When in Rome . . . eat pizza.

31   A bird in the hand is . . . probably going to poop on you.

32   A closed mouth catches no flies . . . it's also a breeding ground for bacteria.

33   A friend in need is . . . a friend whose calls you should screen.

34.   A penny saved is . . . pretty darn useless in this economy.

35   All's well that ends well . . . before your favorite TV show comes on.

36 Beggars can't be choosers . . . or be sticking those Styrofoam cups in your face because that's just plain annoying.

37 Better late than never . . . unless it's your Visa bill in the mail.

38 Blood is thicker than water . . . but so is mustard.

39 Children should be seen and not heard . . . or allowed in restaurants.

40 Don't look a gift horse in the mouth . . . and don't look it in the rear either.

41 Let sleeping dogs lie . . . unless they're lying on your shirt.

42 Time heals all wounds . . . but stitches are more sanitary.

43 Honesty is the best policy . . . except when it can get you in trouble.

44 Necessity is the mother of invention . . . but we still don't know who the father is.

45 Laughter is the best medicine . . . unless you have some real serious disease, in which case you should call a doctor.

46 Rome was not built in a day . . . it probably took at least two.

47 The more the merrier . . . unless you don't have enough hors d'oeuvres to go around.

48 Those who can't do, teach . . . and they can't even do that right.

49 Still waters run deep . . . and that's where the killer sharks hang out.

50   You are what you eat . . . so it's best not to eat elephants and rats and stuff like that.

51   Don't bite the hand that feeds you . . . lick it.

52   Two heads are better than one . . . unless you own only one hat.

53   You cannot make a silk purse out of a sow's ear . . . but then again, why would you want to?

54   If you don't have something nice to say about someone . . . whisper it really low, so they can't hear you.

APPENDIX E

The Smart Girl's Top Five Lists

• TOP FIVE PRESENTS IT IS ABSOLUTELY OKAY TO RE-GIFT •

1. An electronic sound spa machine.

2. Any decorative candle.

3. A food gift basket (but eat all the good stuff first—just pass on the stuff you don't want).

4. Place mat sets.

5. Christmas tree ornaments.

• TOP FIVE LINES GUARANTEED TO END AN UNWANTED CONVERSATION •

1. "Would you excuse me . . . I have to change my tampon."

2. "Hey, I really like you. Wanna have a sleepover? We can stay up late, braid each other's hair and do séances to contact the dead."

③ "Well, it's a loooooooong story. I'll start at the beginning. . . . First, I was born."

④ "Are there two of you? Because I'm seeing double since I changed my meds."

⑤ "I'm dying."

• TOP FIVE REVENGE MOVIES •

① *Basic Instinct*

② *Fatal Attraction*

③ *The Terminator*

④ *Thelma & Louise*

⑤ *The Godfather: I, II, III*

• TOP FIVE REVENGE MEALS •

① Chili

② Tuna fish sandwich

③ Day-old sushi

④ Chilled monkey brains

⑤ A pomegranate

• TOP FIVE WEAPONS OF MASS REVENGE •

① Bad breath

② Body odor

③ Contagious skin rashes

④ Boogers

⑤ Gas

APPENDIX F

Before You Meet Your Maker

Sad but true, you are going to eventually . . . er, shall we say, pass on? Slip to the other side . . . kick the bucket . . . mosey on through the white light . . . meet your Maker . . . keel over and . . . well, we're just gonna say it here, mince no words. . . .

Darling, eventually you are going to DIE.

But fear not. Whether you are stomped to death by a gaggle of wild geese or drowned on a kayaking expedition, even an appointment with the good ol' Grim Reaper has its advantages. For being dead means you can exact revenge on your nemeses without fear of consequence.

So, if you cross against the light, get hit by a bus, and find yourself walking toward that white light one day next week, don't spend your final moments alive feeling sorry for yourself or saying good-bye to loved ones. Have some fun on your deathbed!

❶ Sign yourself up for every "6 CDs for only 49 cents" club known to man.

❷ Charge a house to your credit card.

❸ Convert to another religion.

❹ Mail a package of steaming dog poop to your boss.

⑤ Hook up illegal cable throughout your entire home.

⑥ Rent every porno movie at the local video store under your brother's name.

⑦ Sign up to volunteer for a three-year stint with the Peace Corps.

⑧ Cancel your health insurance policy.

⑨ Write a bunch of bad checks.

⑩ Leave strict instructions in your Will that you be given an elaborate funeral at your family's expense—complete with dancing elephants and a giant chocolate fondue fountain.

ACKNOWLEDGMENTS

I would not be here today, quite literally, were it not for my parents, Jeff and Jennifer Grambs, who are foolish enough to claim me as their daughter. Some children search high and low for worthy role models, but I never had to look further than across the dining room table for mine—or in the utility closet, if Mom and Dad were doing laundry. So blessed am I to have such devoted, brainy, witty, adventurous, worldly, and ethical parents guiding me through the ups and downs of life. They embrace my myriad flaws, support my most dim-witted endeavors, and always know what to say to make me feel better on a bad day—even if it's a complete lie. I thank them from the upper left corner of my spleen for a life filled with so much love and laughter, and would simply be lost in this world without them.

I would also be lost without my oh-so brave, loving and hunky husband, Tommy Schwing, who will never understand how truly remarkable he is. Durka, Durka. He protects me from the purple monsters of the world, and makes me laugh every day. A better motorcycling/ATV-ing/road tripping/camping/scuba diving buddy I could not ask for, and it is a privilege to come home to him every day—even when he hasn't done the dishes. Thanks also to all 587 members of his fun-loving family.

My immeasurable gratitude goes to Citadel Press—particularly, my wonderfully witty and visionary editor, Danielle Chiotti, the ultimate Smart Girl. I am forever indebted to her for giving me the opportunity to write the book of my dreams, and every writer should have the pleasure of working with such a knowledgeable and creative editor. (This project was so much more fun than writing a treatise on the history of dust, which was my other option.) I also pledge allegiance to my agent, Grace Freedson, who saw something in me years ago and, though it must have frightened her terribly, still took me on. It is an honor to have a woman of such integrity steering my career, and I owe her lunch for like, four hundred years. Huge hugs also go to Ken and Gerry Greengrass, who paved the way for me in so many ways, and are like family to me . . . only not as annoying.

And then there's the New York Friars Club—my comedy graduate school of sorts. Jean Pierre Trebot, Freddie Roman, Michael Caputo, Frank Capitelli, Stu Cantor, the incomparable members, and stellar staff from the basement on up to the 6th Floor—you are my second family, and I thank you all for a sinfully fun job that envelops me with so much humor and support on a daily basis. I also thank you for not making me wear pantyhose.

Now, a Smart Girl knows she is nothing without her equally smart friends, and the following individuals have impacted my life in ways they cannot possibly imagine: Lydia Martinez & Patricia Quindoy—my guardian angels, who truly make this world a better place; Alexis Christoforous & Emily Carroll—the sisters I never had, and the therapists I often need; Barry Dougherty & Luisa Buchell—my very funny, very demented partners in crime; Brian Allas & Janet Stafford—my beloved amigos; Stu & Maria Chassen—the hosts with the most; and Valerie Sterlacci & Jason Militello—who are cooler than any NASCAR drivers. Thanks also to David "Gramps" Grambs, Chicago City Limits, Bill Britten, Marvin Scott, Ges Selmont, and Rob Schiffmann—they know why. And if they don't, well, that's not my problem.

And lastly, I wish to thank my favorite writers and comics, who shall remain nameless for fear of a lawsuit. Suffice it to say, some have the letters "B," "K," or "C" in their names, and some have the letters "O," "N," or "P." One of them, a brilliant, and most kind mentor from whom my verbose self has learned so much, has an A-L-A-N in his first name, and a Z-W-E-I-B-E-L in his last. But none of them has an "X" or that weird looking "Û" thing. Anyway, the works of these artists are an inspiration . . . as well as a constant reminder that I have no talent whatsoever.